ALSO BY AMERICA'S TEST KITCHEN

Five-Ingredient Dinners

The Complete Autumn and Winter Cookbook

One-Hour Comfort

The Complete Salad Cookbook

Cooking for One

Cook for Your Gut Health

The Complete Plant-Based Cookbook

The Ultimate Meal-Prep Cookbook

How Can It Be Gluten Free Cookbook Collection

The Complete One Pot

Meat Illustrated

Vegetables Illustrated

The Complete Summer Cookbook

Bowls

The Chicken Bible

The Side Dish Bible

Foolproof Fish

100 Techniques

Easy Everyday Keto

Everything Chocolate

The Perfect Pie

The Perfect Cake

The Perfect Cookie

Bread Illustrated

How to Cocktail

Spiced

The Ultimate Burger

The New Essentials Cookbook

Dinner Illustrated

America's Test Kitchen Menu Cookbook

Cook's Illustrated Revolutionary Recipes

Tasting Italy: A Culinary Journey

Cooking at Home with Bridget and Julia

The Complete Mediterranean Cookbook

The Complete Cooking for Two Cookbook

The Complete Diabetes Cookbook

The Complete Slow Cooker

The Complete Make-Ahead Cookbook

The Complete Vegetarian Cookbook

Just Add Sauce

How to Braise Everything

How to Roast Everything

Nutritious Delicious

What Good Cooks Know

Cook's Science

The Science of Good Cooking

Master of the Grill

Kitchen Smarts

Kitchen Hacks

100 Recipes: The Absolute Best Ways to Make the True Essentials

The New Family Cookbook

The America's Test Kitchen Cooking School Cookbook

The Cook's Illustrated Baking Book

The Cook's Illustrated Cookbook

The America's Test Kitchen Family Baking Book

America's Test Kitchen Twentieth Anniversary TV Show Cookbook

The Best of America's Test Kitchen (2007–2022 Editions)

The Complete America's Test Kitchen TV Show Cookbook 2001–2022

Toaster Oven Perfection

Mediterranean Instant Pot

Cook It in Your Dutch Oven

Vegan for Everybody

Sous Vide for Everybody

Air Fryer Perfection

Multicooker Perfection

Food Processor Perfection

Pressure Cooker Perfection

Instant Pot Ace Blender Cookbook

Naturally Sweet

Foolproof Preserving

Paleo Perfected

The Best Mexican Recipes

Slow Cooker Revolution Volume 2: The Easy-Prep Edition

Slow Cooker Revolution

The America's Test Kitchen D.I.Y. Cookbook

THE COOK'S ILLUSTRATED ALL-TIME BEST SERIES

All-Time Best Brunch

All-Time Best Dinners for Two

All-Time Best Sunday Suppers

All-Time Best Holiday Entertaining

All-Time Best Soups

COOK'S COUNTRY TITLES

Big Flavors from Italian America

One-Pan Wonders

Cook It in Cast Iron

Cook's Country Eats Local

The Complete Cook's Country TV Show Cookbook

FOR A FULL LISTING OF ALL OUR BOOKS

CooksIllustrated.com

AmericasTestKitchen.com

PRAISE FOR AMERICA'S TEST KITCHEN TITLES

"The book's depth, breadth, and practicality makes it a must-have for seafood lovers."
PUBLISHERS WEEKLY (STARRED REVIEW) ON FOOLPROOF FISH

"Another flawless entry in the America's Test Kitchen canon, *Bowls* guides readers of all culinary skill levels in composing one-bowl meals from a variety of cuisines."
BUZZFEED BOOKS ON BOWLS

"If there's room in the budget for one multicooker/ Instant Pot cookbook, make it this one."
BOOKLIST ON MULTICOOKER PERFECTION

"This book upgrades slow cooking for discriminating, 21st century palates—that is indeed revolutionary."
THE DALLAS MORNING NEWS ON SLOW COOKER REVOLUTION

"This book begins with a detailed buying guide, a critical summary of available sizes and attachments, and a list of clever food processor techniques. Easy and versatile dishes follow. . . . Both new and veteran food processor owners will love this practical guide."
LIBRARY JOURNAL ON FOOD PROCESSOR PERFECTION

Selected as the Cookbook Award Winner of 2019 in the Health and Special Diet Category
INTERNATIONAL ASSOCIATION OF CULINARY PROFESSIONALS (IACP) ON THE COMPLETE DIABETES COOKBOOK

"*The Perfect Cookie* . . . is, in a word, perfect. This is an important and substantial cookbook. . . . If you love cookies, but have been a tad shy to bake on your own, all your fears will be dissipated. This is one book you can use for years with magnificently happy results."
THE HUFFINGTON POST ON THE PERFECT COOKIE

"The book offers an impressive education for curious cake makers, new and experienced alike. A summation of 25 years of cake making at ATK, there are cakes for every taste."
THE WALL STREET JOURNAL ON THE PERFECT CAKE

"The sum total of exhaustive experimentation . . . anyone interested in gluten-free cookery simply shouldn't be without it."
NIGELLA LAWSON ON THE HOW CAN IT BE GLUTEN-FREE COOKBOOK

"If you're a home cook who loves long introductions that tell you why a dish works followed by lots of step-by-step hand holding, then you'll love *Vegetables Illustrated*."
THE WALL STREET JOURNAL ON VEGETABLES ILLUSTRATED

"True to its name, this smart and endlessly enlightening cookbook is about as definitive as it's possible to get in the modern vegetarian realm."
MEN'S JOURNAL ON THE COMPLETE VEGETARIAN COOKBOOK

"A one-volume kitchen seminar, addressing in one smart chapter after another the sometimes surprising whys behind a cook's best practices. . . . You get the myth, the theory, the science, and the proof, all rigorously interrogated as only America's Test Kitchen can do."
NPR ON THE SCIENCE OF GOOD COOKING

"The 21st-century *Fannie Farmer Cookbook* or *The Joy of Cooking*. If you had to have one cookbook and that's all you could have, this one would do it."
CBS SAN FRANCISCO ON THE NEW FAMILY COOKBOOK

"Some 2,500 photos walk readers through 600 painstakingly tested recipes, leaving little room for error."
ASSOCIATED PRESS ON THE AMERICA'S TEST KITCHEN COOKING SCHOOL COOKBOOK

"The go-to gift book for newlyweds, small families, or empty nesters."
ORLANDO SENTINEL ON THE COMPLETE COOKING FOR TWO COOKBOOK

"Some books impress by the sheer audacity of their ambition. Backed by the magazine's famed mission to test every recipe relentlessly until it is the best it can be, this nearly 900-page volume lands with an authoritative wallop."
CHICAGO TRIBUNE ON THE COOK'S ILLUSTRATED COOKBOOK

"It might become your 'cooking school,' the only book you'll need to make you a proficient cook, recipes included. . . . You can master the 100 techniques with the easy-to-understand instructions, then apply the skill with the recipes that follow."
THE LITCHFIELD COUNTY TIMES ON 100 TECHNIQUES

AMERICA'S TEST KITCHEN

HEALTHY& DELICIOUS INSTANT POT®

INSPIRED MEALS WITH A WORLD OF FLAVOR

AMERICA'S TEST KITCHEN

Instant Pot® and associated logos are owned by Instant Brands Inc. and are used under license.

Library of Congress Cataloging-in-Publication Data
Names: America's Test Kitchen (Firm), author.
Title: Healthy and delicious Instant Pot : inspired meals with a world of flavor / America's Test Kitchen.
Description: Boston, MA : America's Test Kitchen, [2021] | Includes index.
Identifiers: LCCN 2021017505 (print) | LCCN 2021017506 (ebook) | ISBN 9781948703703 (hardcover) | ISBN 9781948703710 (ebook)
Subjects: LCSH: Smart cookers. | Pressure cooking. | Electric cooking. | LCGFT: Cookbooks.
Classification: LCC TX840.S63 A44 2021 (print) | LCC TX840.S63 (ebook) | DDC 641.5/87--dc23
LC record available at https://lccn.loc.gov/2021017505
LC ebook record available at https://lccn.loc.gov/2021017506

America's Test Kitchen
21 Drydock Avenue, Boston, MA 02210

Printed in Canada

10 9 8 7 6 5 4 3 2 1

Distributed by Penguin Random House Publisher Services
Tel: 800.733.3000

Pictured on front cover **Smoky Paprika Rice with Crispy Artichokes and Peppers (page 162)**

Pictured on back cover **Chipotle Chicken and Black Beans with Pickled Cabbage (page 38); Spaghetti and Turkey Meatballs (page 168); Shredded Chicken Tacos with Mango Salsa (page 57); Hawaiian Oxtail Soup (page 66)**

Featured Photography **Joseph Keller**
Featured Food Styling **Catrine Kelty**

Editorial Director, Books **Adam Kowit**
Executive Food Editor **Dan Zuccarello**
Deputy Food Editor **Stephanie Pixley**
Executive Managing Editor **Debra Hudak**
Senior Editors **Sam Block, Sarah Ewald, Joseph Gitter, and Nicole Konstantinakos**
Editor **Emily Rahravan**
Assistant Editor **Sara Zatopek**
Design Director **Lindsey Timko Chandler**
Deputy Art Director **Janet Taylor**
Designer **Molly Gillespie**
Photography Director **Julie Bozzo Cote**
Photography Producer **Meredith Mulcahy**
Senior Staff Photographers **Steve Klise and Daniel J. van Ackere**
Staff Photographer **Kevin White**
Photoshoot Kitchen Team
Photo Team and Special Events Manager **Alli Berkey**
Lead Test Cook **Eric Haessler**
Test Cooks **Hannah Fenton, Jacqueline Gochenouer, and Gina McCreadie**
Assistant Test Cooks **Hisham Hassan and Christa West**
Senior Manager, Publishing Operations **Taylor Argenzio**
Imaging Manager **Lauren Robbins**
Production and Imaging Specialists **Tricia Neumyer, Dennis Noble, and Amanda Yong**
Copy Editor **Jeffrey Schier**
Proofreader **Vicki Rowland**
Indexer **Elizabeth Parson**

Chief Creative Officer **Jack Bishop**
Executive Editorial Directors **Julia Collin Davison and Bridget Lancaster**

CONTENTS

ix   Welcome to America's Test Kitchen

x   Getting Started

21   Chicken

63   Beef, Pork, and Lamb

97   Seafood

131   Vegetables and Grains

167   Pasta and Noodles

194   Nutritional Information for Our Recipes

198   Conversions and Equivalents

200   Index

WELCOME TO AMERICA'S TEST KITCHEN

This book has been tested, written, and edited by the folks at America's Test Kitchen, where curious cooks become confident cooks. Located in Boston's Seaport District in the historic Innovation and Design Building, it features 15,000 square feet of kitchen space, including multiple photography and video studios. It is the home of *Cook's Illustrated* magazine and *Cook's Country* magazine and is the workday destination for more than 60 test cooks, editors, and cookware specialists. Our mission is to empower and inspire confidence, community, and creativity in the kitchen.

We start the process of testing a recipe with a complete lack of preconceptions, which means that we accept no claim, no technique, and no recipe at face value. We simply assemble as many variations as possible, test a half-dozen of the most promising, and taste the results blind. We then construct our own recipe and continue to test it, varying ingredients, techniques, and cooking times, until we reach a consensus. As we like to say in the test kitchen, "We make the mistakes so you don't have to." The result, we hope, is the best version of a particular recipe, but we realize that only you can be the final judge of our success (or failure). We use the same rigorous approach when we test equipment and taste ingredients.

All of this would not be possible without a belief that good cooking, much like good music, is based on a foundation of objective technique. Some people like spicy foods and others don't, but there is a right way to sauté, there is a best way to cook a pot roast, and there are measurable scientific principles involved in producing perfectly beaten, stable egg whites. Our ultimate goal is to investigate the fundamental principles of cooking to give you the techniques, tools, and ingredients you need to become a better cook. It is as simple as that.

To see what goes on behind the scenes at America's Test Kitchen, check out our social media channels for kitchen snapshots, exclusive content, video tips, and much more. You can watch us work (in our actual test kitchen) by tuning in to *America's Test Kitchen* or *Cook's Country* on public television or on our websites. Listen to *Proof*, *Mystery Recipe*, and *The Walk-In* (AmericasTestKitchen.com/podcasts) to hear engaging, complex stories about people and food. Want to hone your cooking skills or finally learn how to bake—with an America's Test Kitchen test cook? Enroll in one of our online cooking classes. And you can engage the next generation of home cooks with kid-tested recipes from America's Test Kitchen Kids.

Our community of home recipe testers provides valuable feedback on recipes under development by ensuring that they are foolproof. You can help us investigate the how and why behind successful recipes from your home kitchen. (Sign up at AmericasTestKitchen.com/recipe_testing.)

However you choose to visit us, we welcome you into our kitchen, where you can stand by our side as we test our way to the best recipes in America.

facebook.com/AmericasTestKitchen

twitter.com/TestKitchen

youtube.com/AmericasTestKitchen

instagram.com/TestKitchen

pinterest.com/TestKitchen

AmericasTestKitchen.com
CooksIllustrated.com
CooksCountry.com
OnlineCookingSchool.com
AmericasTestKitchen.com/kids

GETTING STARTED

1 Introduction

2 Healthy Doesn't Have to Be Hard

3 Useful Tools and Helpful Tips

4 Inside the Pot

5 Troubleshooting

6 Your Instant Pot Workshop

8 Cooking Rice and Grains

10 Cooking Beans and Lentils

11 Cooking Vegetables

12 Cooking Proteins

14 Sauces and Dressings

18 Toppings and Sprinkles

INTRODUCTION

When the Instant Pot hit the market in 2010 it was a near-immediate success, and its sales and popularity have been on an upward trajectory ever since. Now, more than a decade later, there are numerous iterations of the device. Older versions are still reliable, while newer ones have stronger heating elements for faster cooking. When we did our first multicooker book, we set our sights on typically long-cooking dishes such as pot roasts and beef stew, wanting to take advantage of the unit's speed. But the more we used the equipment, the more we wanted to explore the fresher side of things. With this in mind, we aimed to deliver recipes that accommodated the new technology while bringing vegetables to the front and knocking flavor out of the park. So, while you will still find a beef stew recipe in this book, you'll also discover that we've doubled down on vegetable content and incorporated lemon zest for a refreshing finish (page 64).

We love the Instant Pot because it doesn't just *make* healthy food, it makes healthy food easier. It can cook multiple components at the same time while seamlessly toggling from browning to pressure cooking to simmering at the touch of a button. We were thrilled we could pressure-poach chicken in a spiced soy sauce and wine broth, then simmer everything and stir in tender Chinese broccoli (page 50); braise short ribs, then lighten the meal by pairing them with nutty cauliflower warmed directly in the braising liquid (page 76); fry sage, sauté garlic in the sage oil, pressure-cook butternut squash and white beans, then turn off the pot and cook shrimp gently in the residual heat (page 125). From braising to boiling, sautéing to searing, the Instant Pot makes healthy cooking exciting and achievable.

Whether you're preparing nutritious à la carte ingredients or complete meals for the whole family, we've got your back on the road to flavorful, low-lift dinners. The Instant Pot is a natural match for healthy food, and our seasoning skills are a natural match to ensure that the food is delicious. Often, you can't open the pot to check on your meal during cooking, so it's vital to have a trustworthy collection of recipes. We put our science minds to the test to ensure cooked to-perfection success in all 75 recipes—guaranteed to work in your pot.

HEALTHY DOESN'T HAVE TO BE HARD

Health-focused food gets a bad reputation for being hassle-inducing. The Instant Pot takes the hassle out of it at every step with its one-pot, multiuse efficiency, and what we promise in ease we can also deliver in flavor.

WHAT WE MEAN BY HEALTHY

We've taken a holistic approach because strict diets and "off-limits food" can leave you desperately craving that which you can't have. No ingredients were forbidden, and instead we based everything on the idea of bountiful, healthful foods for balanced meals. Instead of simply making low-calorie swaps, our test cooks crafted easy-to-execute recipes with nutrient-dense ingredients and seasoned them expertly. We flipped the traditional ratio on its head so that meals focus on upping vegetable content and keeping protein amounts moderate. No hard rules, just easy eating. So why the Instant Pot?

First, it speeds up long-cooking, nutritious ingredients such as vitamin-rich oat berries and antioxidant-full black rice (which we all would like to eat more of). While these foods can take over an hour on the stovetop, the Instant Pot cuts cooking to a fraction of the time and makes the process fairly hands-off.

Second, it is precise and foolproof. The Instant Pot lets you set the exact heat, time, and mode you want for your cooking. With tested and approved recipes and a calibrated piece of machinery, you can't go wrong.

Third, the Instant Pot eliminates extensive cleanup, as all cooking is done in one contained vessel. No more juggling multiple pots and pans, and no dreaded equipment pile in the sink that needs to be washed after dinner.

NO BORING FOOD

Health food isn't all grilled chicken breast, steamed veggies, and brown rice. We were inspired by a wide range of cuisines, and we expanded our idea of what makes a meal exciting. We broke oatmeal down to its basics to discover that it goes beyond breakfast and could also be a creamy, savory dinner porridge full of mushrooms and fried leeks (page 164). We brought our favorite fast-casual Tex-Mex bowl home by swapping out rice for hearty oat berries, then pairing them with charred poblanos and garlic shrimp and topping everything with a heap of fresh avocado, bright corn salsa, salty tortilla chips, and a spicy chipotle-yogurt sauce (page 122). No matter the cuisine, whether Mexican, French, Italian, Persian, Spanish, or any other, we kept our ingredient lists thorough but not overwhelming so you'll look forward to every meal.

USEFUL TOOLS

We reach for various tools time and time again when working with the Instant Pot. Though these are not *necessary* to complete our recipes, they can help you do so successfully.

	TOOL	NOTES
	Tongs	The Instant Pot is narrow and can get very hot, so we prefer these as our primary reaching-in and flipping tool.
	Fat separator	We love the flavor imparted by fatty meats, but we don't love the unhealthy grease. By defatting many of our recipes we could keep the flavor for cooking but remove the fat for eating.
	Digital scale	When cooking in an Instant Pot, it is vital to follow specs exactly, as this is how cook times are calibrated. A digital scale ensures proteins are exactly the right weight, avoiding over- or undercooking.
	Flexible spatula with offset handle	This instrument aids in easily getting food out of the high-sided chamber, and it can be used to press food down against the cooking surface to get a distinct sear.
	Wooden utensil	This tool is ideal for dislodging any stuck food and fond because it does not damage the interior pot. This is particularly important with newer models and their extra-powerful heating element.
	Soufflé dish	Perfect for cooking polenta in the Instant Pot, this dish keeps the polenta contained for easy cooking and mess-free removal.

HELPFUL TIPS

We endured the trials and tribulations so you don't have to; here are some tips to keep in mind.

TIP	NOTES
Mind the moat	The shape of the interior pot bottom will affect cooking. New pots have a flat bottom cooking surface, while older iterations have a rounded middle that can produce a "moat" around the inside perimeter. When sautéing in the older models, stir well to avoid oil pooling to the outside of the pot, away from the food.
Hot button issue	New models require you to manually press "start" after setting the cook functions (for sauté level, pressure function, time, etc.), while older pots will start cooking automatically once you have selected your cooking functions. If you have a new model, be sure to hit "start" to kick off cooking; otherwise you may sit around waiting for food to cook in a cold pot.
Read up	Look to your manual for understanding error messages, which can occur for a variety of model-specific reasons. Your manual can help you determine why these are happening in your exact pot. If you have misplaced the manual, there are almost always free PDFs available online; simply search for your model type.

INSIDE THE POT

We developed this book using the Instant Pot because it is the most widely owned electric pressure cooker and offers numerous new models and updated features. By testing on pots new and old, we were able to account for model differences by factoring in adjusted cook times and modifying our release methods within recipe steps.

DEMYSTIFY THE POT

So, what does a pressure cooker do? In a sealed pot under pressure, the boiling point of liquid is higher. Normally, water turns to steam at 212°F. In a closed environment, water molecules can't escape, so the interior pressure increases. More energy is needed for the water to boil, so the temperature in the pot increases. This means that you are cooking with steam that's at a temperature up to 34 degrees higher than what's possible in a normal pot; AKA, shorter cooking times.

KNOW YOUR HEATING ELEMENTS

The updated heating element on newer models means that sautéed or browned items cook more quickly. This led us to test on an array of pots to standardize our recipes and provide a range of cook times. A recipe may say to "cook for 3 to 5 minutes." The shorter end of the range is likely to be sufficient to achieve the desired result in newer models, while you can rely on the longer end of the range in older models.

IGNORE PRESET FUNCTIONS

Preset functions are a preprogrammed combination specifying the amount of heat, time, and pressure the pot is to use. To make our recipes foolproof, and to account for model differences, we prescribe manually selecting what is required for all three variables to ensure perfect cooking.

UNDERSTAND HIGH VS. LOW PRESSURE

The Instant Pot has two pressure levels. Most recipes use high pressure for its efficiency. We use low pressure for dried bean recipes where texture is vital.

THE DIFFERENCE IN RELEASE TECHNIQUES

There are two methods for releasing pressure after cooking. Each affects the final outcome of a recipe, so don't swap one for the other. Most important, don't force the Instant Pot open before the pressure has been fully released.

WHEN TO USE NATURAL RELEASE

This is the preferred method to finish cooking gently, since the contents will continue to cook as the pressure drops. The release method can also affect texture: Natural release is ideal for most beans because it reduces blowouts. After 15 minutes of natural release, we quick-release any remaining pressure.

WHEN TO USE QUICK RELEASE

To release pressure immediately, turn the pressure regulator knob to "vent" as soon as your recipe is done cooking. We use quick release when we want to stop cooking right away and prevent overcooking in delicate recipes such as Haddock with Tomatoes, Escarole, and Crispy Garlic (page 114).

TROUBLESHOOTING

In the test kitchen we embrace setbacks, because they bring us closer to achieving foolproof recipes. After spending months in the kitchen with our Instant Pots, we came up with a few key tricks to fix the common problems we encountered.

PROBLEM	SOLUTION	NOTES
Undercooked food	Continue to cook the food using the highest sauté function or residual heat	Since it's impossible to test the doneness of food as it cooks under pressure, sometimes it might be slightly underdone. Finish cooking by partially covering the pot, switching to the highest sauté function, and adding extra liquid if needed. For some fish recipes, we simply cover the turned-off pot and let it sit in the residual heat.
Uneven cooking	Prep ingredients as directed	There's no undoing an unevenly cooked dish, but to ensure better results next time, be sure that your ingredients are prepped properly: Buy fish within the thickness range we call for, measure liquids accurately, and grab a ruler when cutting veggies. Arranging the ingredients in an even layer also helps prevent unevenness.
Sauce is too thick, or too thin	Add more liquid, or continue to simmer (or let it rest)	Sauces that are too thin can be simmered uncovered on the highest sauté function to thicken up before serving, and thick sauces can be thinned out with additional broth or water. Keep in mind that many dishes may look a little watery when you open the lid, but a brief rest allows them to thicken up (especially pasta dishes).
Scorching during cooking	Add additional liquid and scrape up browned bits	We ensured that the recipes in this book contain enough liquid to prevent scorching, but keep an eye out when using your own recipes. If you experience burning while sautéing, try adding a small amount of liquid. Although you can't fix food that has been burned during pressure cooking, you can avoid the problem in the future by scraping up all the browned bits left in the pot after sautéing food and before closing the lid. An improperly sealed lid can also cause the Instant Pot to continue to release steam as it attempts to reach pressure, and this will lead to scorching.
Never reaching pressure	Check the silicone gasket and pressure regulating knob	If your Instant Pot is not coming to pressure, it may not be sealed correctly. Check that the silicone gasket around the bottom lip of the lid is not cracked or improperly installed, and be sure that the pressure regulating knob (on the lid) is in the closed position.
Burn message	Depressurize and inspect; add liquid	This indicates overheating. When a high temperature is detected under the inner pot, the burn-protection mechanism suspends heating to avoid burning food. In denser dishes (rice and grains), or in dishes with thicker sauces, sometimes the available liquid is pushed to the top while the solids settle to the bottom, causing overheating. Stir to recombine or add more liquid if necessary.
C8 error message	Make sure the bottom of your cooking insert is clean	On some models, debris or even water on the bottom of your pot can generate a C8 error message, indicating that an improper insert is being used, and the system shuts down.

YOUR INSTANT POT WORKSHOP

The Instant Pot is the ideal vessel for preparing healthy ingredients, as it gives you a head start for the rest of your cooking, which may require more active attention (and time). Your Instant Pot can make anything from fluffy wild rice and poached salmon to crisp-tender broccoli. Consider it your personal cooking workshop equipped to produce exactly what you need, à la carte. To really round out your dishes and bring everything together, top with your favorite sauce. Although everything can be made ahead and stored, bases and beans reheat best, so you may consider cooking those in advance and preparing some time-sensitive proteins or a few delicate vegetables the day they will be consumed.

1 ALWAYS HAVE SNACKS ON HAND
Use your pot to make quick and satisfying items like hard-cooked eggs, crisp-tender vegetables, or beans tossed with spices for a simple snack

2 MAKE BASES IN ADVANCE TO BUILD A BOWL
Rice, grains, and beans cook in a flash, store easily, and reheat well for whatever your need may be

3 GET A LEG UP ON INTERESTING SALADS
Adding cooked vegetables to any salad can boost flavor, nutrition, visual appearance, and textural contrast

4 ADD A PROTEIN
Sometimes all you need is a well-cooked piece of fish to flake over a salad, or some cooked chicken to shred into enchiladas

5 FINISH WITH A CRUNCH
No matter what you make in your Instant Pot, a crunchy component can really set any meal apart and put it over the top

COOKING RICE AND GRAINS

The Instant Pot is the best way to cook big batches of rice or grains to have on hand to combine with other recipes or to round out any meal. They store easily and reheat reliably, and it's simple to jazz them up. Try fluffing in some flavored oil, fresh herbs, or any other flavorful ingredients such as toasted nuts or grated cheese. We developed our chart recipes and timing using the Instant Pot Pro and Duo Plus models. Results may vary slightly if using a different model.

TIPS FOR PREPARATION

Rinse First Rice and grains are typically coated with a thin dusting of starch. This coating should be rinsed away before cooking to keep the rice and grains from clumping together, and to prevent the cooking water from turning overly starchy and foamy, which can clog the pressure-release valve. To rinse your rice and grains, place them in a fine-mesh strainer set under running water and stir with your hand until the water runs clear. (Exceptions are recipes where we want the starches to add texture to the dish, such as risotto.)

Add a Little Oil Always add oil when cooking either rice or grains, as this helps the individual grains remain more distinct and clump less. Oil also helps reduce the amount of starchy foam.

Use Enough Water Having enough water in the pot is crucial for even cooking. We use the boil method for heartier grains that can withstand a more vigorous cooking process. The amount of water also affects the time it takes for the pot to come to pressure and the cooking time; don't be tempted to adjust the water amounts.

COOKING INSTRUCTIONS

For Pilaf Method Rinse 1½ cups rice or grains, then combine in Instant Pot with water amount indicated in chart, 1 tablespoon oil, and ½ teaspoon table salt. Lock lid into place and close pressure-release valve. Select high pressure-cook function and set cook time according to chart. Turn off Instant Pot and quick-release pressure. Carefully remove lid, allowing steam to escape away from you. Fluff rice or grains gently with fork. Lay clean dish towel over pot, replace lid, and let sit for 5 minutes. Makes about 4 cups.

For Boil Method Rinse 1½ cups rice or grains, then combine in Instant Pot with water amount indicated in chart, 1 tablespoon oil, and 1½ teaspoons table salt. (When cooking wheat berries reduce salt to ½ teaspoon.) Lock lid into place and close pressure-release valve. Select high pressure-cook function and set cook time according to chart. Turn off Instant Pot and let pressure release naturally for 15 minutes. Quick-release any remaining pressure, then carefully remove lid, allowing steam to escape away from you. Drain cooked rice or grains through fine-mesh strainer. Makes about 4 cups. (To make smaller batch, decrease amount of rice or grains, but keep same amounts of water, oil, and salt.)

RICE/GRAIN	COOKING METHOD	WATER AMOUNT	COOK TIME	RELEASE TYPE
long-grain white rice	pilaf	2 cups	6 minutes	quick
long-grain brown rice	pilaf	2⅓ cups	22 minutes	quick
wild rice	boil	8 cups	15 minutes	natural
black rice	pilaf	2⅓ cups	18 minutes	quick
barley, pearled	boil	8 cups	4 minutes	natural
bulgur, medium-grind	pilaf	2⅓ cups	1 minute	quick
farro	boil	8 cups	1 minute*	natural
oat berries (groats)	boil	8 cups	20 minutes	natural
wheat berries	boil	8 cups	30 minutes	natural
quinoa	pilaf	1¾ cups	8 minutes	quick
pearl couscous	pilaf	2¼ cups	6 minutes	quick

*Set cook time for 1 minute; as soon as Instant Pot reaches pressure, turn it off.

MAKE THEM AHEAD

Rice and grains can be cooked, cooled, and then refrigerated in an airtight container for up to 3 days. To reheat, microwave in a covered bowl until hot, fluffing with a fork halfway through microwaving, then season to taste. (Reheating time will vary depending on the quantity and type of rice or grains.) Alternatively, enjoy cooked rice or grains cold or at room temperature, tossed with a vinaigrette or drizzled with a fresh sauce.

COOKING BEANS AND LENTILS

The Instant Pot makes quick work of cooking dried beans and lentils, which are in protein, vitamins, and minerals and are a great way to bulk up the nutritional content of any dish or recipe. The high-pressure environment infuses them with whatever flavors you add to the cooking liquid (such as hearty herbs, citrus zest, or garlic).

TIPS FOR PREPARATION

Brine the Beans Brining dried beans before cooking is crucial for texture and minimizes busted beans. (It's not necessary for lentils.) Brine 1 pound of beans overnight (or up to 24 hours in advance) in 2 quarts cold water plus 1½ tablespoons table salt. If you are short on time, you can "quick-brine" your beans: Combine water, salt, and beans in the pot, bring to boil using the high sauté function, then turn off the pot and let sit for 1 hour. Drain and rinse beans after brining.

Add a Little Oil Always add oil to the cooking liquid to help prevent foaming.

Use Low Pressure & Natural Release (Usually)
Cooking beans and lentils under low pressure promotes more even cooking. We mostly use natural release after cooking beans, but we use quick release for brown or green lentils.

COOKING INSTRUCTIONS

Combine 1 pound brined beans or 2 cups lentils in Instant Pot with 8 cups water, 1 tablespoon extra-virgin olive oil, and ½ teaspoon table salt. Lock lid into place and close pressure-release valve. Select low pressure-cook function and set cook time according to chart. Turn off Instant Pot when done and quick-release pressure (except for French green lentils). Carefully remove lid, allowing steam to escape away from you. Remove any floating beans or lentils. Drain cooked beans or lentils through fine-mesh strainer.

MAKE THEM AHEAD

Beans and legumes can be cooked, cooled, and then refrigerated in an airtight container for up to 3 days. To reheat, microwave in a covered bowl until hot, stirring gently halfway through microwaving, then season to taste. (Reheating time will vary depending on the quantity and type of beans or lentils.) Alternatively, enjoy cooked beans or lentils cold or at room temperature, tossed with a vinaigrette or drizzled with a fresh sauce.

BEAN TYPE	COOK TIME	RELEASE TYPE
black beans	1 minute*	natural
black-eyed peas	1 minute*	natural
cannellini beans	4 minutes	natural
chickpeas	1 minute	natural
great northern beans	1 minute	natural
kidney beans	3 minutes	natural
navy beans	1 minute	natural
pinto beans	3 minutes	natural
small red beans	3 minutes	natural
French green lentils (lentilles du Puy)	1 minute*	natural
brown/green lentils	3 minutes	quick

*As soon as pressure is reached, turn off Instant Pot.

COOKING VEGETABLES

This chart provides general cook times for you to build and customize your own dishes with well-cooked vegetables. Make your favorite veggies in advance so that at any time you're just moments away from a nutritious, delicious meal. These times (with quick pressure release) are just a starting point and can vary depending on how you cut the vegetables and what else you add to the pot. You will need to add a minimum of ½ cup of liquid for the pot to reach pressure.

VEGETABLE	COOK TIME
1½ pounds unpeeled beets, scrubbed, trimmed, and cut into ½-inch wedges	10 minutes
1½ pounds butternut squash, peeled, seeded, and cut into 1-inch pieces	6 minutes
1½ pounds green or red cabbage, cored and sliced into 1-inch wedges	3 minutes
1½ pounds carrots, peeled and cut into 3-inch lengths, larger pieces halved lengthwise	1 minute
1½ pounds celery root, peeled and cut into 1-inch pieces	5 minutes
1½ pounds broccoli or cored cauliflower, cut into 2-inch florets	1 minute
1½ pounds collard greens or kale, stemmed and cut into 1-inch pieces	3 minutes
1½ pounds green beans, trimmed	1 minute*
1½ pounds red or Yukon Gold potatoes, unpeeled, cut into 1-inch pieces	8 minutes
1½ pounds sweet potatoes, peeled and cut into 1-inch pieces	4 minutes
1½ pounds zucchini or summer squash, halved lengthwise and cut into 1-inch pieces	1 minute

*As soon as pressure is reached, turn off Instant Pot.

MAKE THEM AHEAD

Vegetables can be cooked, cooled, and then refrigerated in an airtight container for up to 3 days. To reheat, microwave in a covered bowl until hot, stirring gently halfway through microwaving, then season to taste. (Reheating time will vary depending on the quantity and type of vegetables.) Because of their high water content, you may prefer to make zucchini and summer squash on the day they are to be used instead of cooking them earlier and reheating; they will reheat fine, though they'll be just a bit mushy. Alternatively, enjoy cooked vegetables cold or at room temperature, tossed with a vinaigrette or drizzled with a fresh sauce.

COOKING PROTEINS

As with the cook times given for vegetables, those listed here are just a starting point and are meant to give you general cooking times as you build your bowls. Having cooked proteins on hand is a great way to avoid that desperate frozen-pizza lunch when hunger strikes and you don't have time to cook. These times can vary depending on what else you add to the Instant Pot. Note that you will need to add a minimum of ½ cup of liquid for the pot to reach pressure.

TIPS FOR PREPARATION

Stick to the Specs To ensure proper cooking, use protein cuts that meet the given specifications. (One exception: If you can't find skinless fish fillets, as long as they meet the specifications for weight and thickness, you can cook the fish with the skin on and remove it after cooking.) See page 3 for information on digital scales.

Quick vs. Natural Release Some proteins are rich in connective tissue (short ribs, lamb shanks, and pork chops), and the natural release method gradually drops the temperature to give the collagen more time to convert to gelatin, producing melt-in-your-mouth meat. Quick release stops the cooking process right away, when you don't want to overdo a delicate protein such as fish.

Browning Adds Flavor But it isn't always necessary! For potently flavored dishes such as Shredded Beef Tacos, we could skip the browning step, but we found it added depth of flavor for simpler dishes like Chicken with Spring Vegetables. And we loved that it could be done using the Instant Pot's sauté function.

Thaw Before Cooking Be sure to thaw any frozen proteins (overnight in the refrigerator) before cooking to ensure they cook properly in the given cook times.

Add Flavor to the Braising Liquid Add some zing and character to your proteins by mixing in your favorite braising sauce, or by adding flavor boosters and aromatics—such as soy sauce, wine, hearty herbs, garlic cloves, fresh ginger, or citrus zest—to the cooking liquid.

Finish with Bright Elements Cooking under pressure is great for intensifying certain flavors, but it can also dull others (many of our recipes call for a greater amount of aromatics than we would specify when cooking on the stovetop), so drizzling the finished dish with your choice of favorite sauce (see pages 14–17) for ideas) or sprinkling it with fresh herbs helps to wake everything up.

Sling It A foil sling makes for easy removal of delicate fish fillets from the pot.

PROTEIN		COOK TIME	RELEASE TYPE
POULTRY	4 (6- to 8-ounce) boneless, skinless chicken breasts, trimmed	4 minutes	quick
	2 (12-ounce) bone-in split chicken breasts, trimmed	10 minutes	quick
	4 (3- to 5-ounce) boneless skinless chicken thighs, trimmed	9 minutes	quick
	4 (5- to 7-ounce) bone-in chicken thighs, trimmed	9 minutes	quick
	1 (4-pound) whole chicken, giblets discarded	24 minutes	quick
MEAT	1 pound boneless beef chuck-eye roast, boneless beef short ribs, or boneless country-style pork ribs, trimmed and cut into 1½-inch pieces	30 minutes	quick
	2 pounds bone-in English-style short ribs, 3 pounds beef oxtails, or 4 (10- to 12-ounce) lamb shanks, trimmed	60 minutes	natural
	4 (8- to 10-ounce) bone-in blade-cut pork chops, about ¾ inch thick, trimmed	10 minutes	natural
	4 (8- to 12-ounce) lamb shoulder chops (blade or round bone), about ¾ inch thick, trimmed	20 minutes	natural
FISH	4 (6-ounce) skinless black sea bass, cod, haddock, hake, pollock, or salmon fillets, 1 to 1½ inches thick	3 minutes	quick
	4 (6-ounce) skinless halibut, mahi-mahi, red snapper, striped bass, or swordfish fillets, 1 to 1½ inches thick	2 minutes	quick
	1 pound squid, bodies sliced crosswise into ¾-inch-thick rings, tentacles halved	20 minutes	quick
	2 pounds littleneck clams, scrubbed	1 minute	quick
	3 pounds mussels, scrubbed and debearded	1 minute*	quick
PLANT-BASED	1 pound tempeh, cut into 1-inch pieces	12 minutes	quick
	1 (14-ounce) block firm tofu, quartered	5 minutes	quick

*Set cook time for 1 minute; as soon as Instant Pot reaches pressure, turn it off and quick-release pressure.

MAKE IT AHEAD

Poultry, meats, fish, and plant-based proteins can be cooked, cooled, and refrigerated in an airtight container for up to 3 days. To reheat, microwave in a covered bowl until hot, then season to taste. Reheating time will vary depending on the quantity and type of protein. Most proteins reheat fine, but certain ones should be made the day of, such as pork chops, to avoid becoming tough. Alternatively, some cooked proteins (for example, seafood and plant-based proteins) can be enjoyed cold or at room temperature, tossed with a vinaigrette or drizzled with a fresh sauce.

SAUCES AND DRESSINGS

Sauces and dressings can enhance any meal, or individual ingredients, you've prepared in your Instant Pot, so turn here to determine the overall flavor profile. Drizzle your sauce of choice over the entire meal, or choose certain elements, such as the protein or vegetables, to be tossed in the liquid as a final dressing to pack a flavorful punch.

POMEGRANATE-HONEY VINAIGRETTE

Makes about 1 cup

This vinaigrette perfectly pairs sweet and tart. To avoid off-flavors, make sure to reduce the fruit juice in a nonreactive stainless-steel saucepan.

2 cups pomegranate juice
1 tablespoon honey
3 tablespoons red wine vinegar
2 tablespoons extra-virgin olive oil
1 tablespoon minced shallot
½ teaspoon table salt
½ teaspoon pepper

Bring pomegranate juice and honey to boil in small saucepan over medium-high heat. Reduce to simmer and cook until thickened and juice measures about ⅔ cup, 15 to 20 minutes. Transfer syrup to medium bowl and refrigerate until cool, about 15 minutes. Whisk in vinegar, oil, shallot, salt, and pepper until combined. (Vinaigrette can be refrigerated for up to 1 week; whisk to recombine before using.)

Apple Cider-Sage Vinaigrette

Substitute apple cider for pomegranate juice, and cider vinegar for red wine vinegar. Add ½ teaspoon minced fresh sage to syrup with vinegar.

Orange-Ginger Vinaigrette

Substitute orange juice for pomegranate juice, and lime juice for red wine vinegar. Add 1 teaspoon grated fresh ginger to syrup with lime juice.

PEANUT-SESAME SAUCE

Makes about ⅔ cup

Peanut butter helps this Asian-inspired sauce turn spectacularly rich and creamy once processed. This simple sauce is perfect to drizzle over a variety of green or grain bowls, including our Chicken and Black Rice Bowl (page 54).

- 3 tablespoons smooth or chunky peanut butter
- 3 tablespoons toasted sesame seeds
- 2 tablespoons soy sauce
- 1½ tablespoons unseasoned rice vinegar
- 1½ tablespoons packed light brown sugar
- 1½ teaspoons grated fresh ginger
- 1 garlic clove, minced
- ¾ teaspoon sriracha

Process all ingredients in blender until smooth and mixture has consistency of heavy cream, about 1 minute (adjust consistency with warm water, 1 tablespoon at a time, as needed). Season with salt and pepper to taste. (Sauce can be refrigerated for up to 3 days; add warm water as needed to loosen before using.)

SRIRACHA-LIME VINAIGRETTE

Makes about 1 cup

This bright, spicy, fresh vinaigrette adds a burst of heat and citrus.

- ¼ cup lime juice (2 limes)
- 2 tablespoons honey
- 2 tablespoons fish sauce
- 1 tablespoon grated fresh ginger
- 1 tablespoon sriracha
- ⅓ cup extra-virgin olive oil

Whisk lime juice, honey, fish sauce, ginger, and sriracha together in medium bowl. While whisking constantly, slowly drizzle in oil until combined. (Vinaigrette can be refrigerated for up to 3 days; whisk to recombine before using.)

MISO-GINGER SAUCE

Makes about ¾ cup

For a thick, saucy dressing packed with flavor, we turned to miso and potent fresh ginger.

- ¼ cup mayonnaise
- 3 tablespoons red miso
- 2 tablespoons water
- 1 tablespoon maple syrup
- 1 tablespoon sesame oil
- 1½ teaspoons sherry vinegar
- 1½ teaspoons grated fresh ginger

Whisk all ingredients together in bowl. (Sauce can be refrigerated for up to 3 days.)

HARISSA

Makes about ½ cup

Harissa is a traditional North African condiment that is great for flavoring soups (like our Chicken Harira on page 24), sauces, and dressings. If Aleppo pepper is unavailable, you can substitute ¾ teaspoon paprika and ¾ teaspoon finely chopped red pepper flakes.

- 6 tablespoons extra-virgin olive oil
- 6 garlic cloves, minced
- 2 tablespoons paprika
- 1 tablespoon ground coriander
- 1 tablespoon ground dried Aleppo pepper
- 1 teaspoon ground cumin
- ¾ teaspoon caraway seeds
- ½ teaspoon table salt

Combine all ingredients in bowl and microwave until bubbling and very fragrant, about 1 minute, stirring halfway through microwaving; let cool to room temperature. (Harissa can be refrigerated for up to 4 days.)

CLASSIC BASIL PESTO

Makes about 1½ cups

This Italian favorite is subject to endless riffing, but we stick to the basics here with floral basil, toasted pine nuts, and fruity olive oil.

- 6 garlic cloves, unpeeled
- ½ cup pine nuts
- 4 cups fresh basil leaves
- ¼ cup fresh parsley leaves
- 1 cup extra-virgin olive oil
- 1 ounce Parmesan cheese, grated fine (½ cup)

1 Toast garlic in 8-inch skillet over medium heat, shaking skillet occasionally, until softened and spotty brown, about 8 minutes. When garlic is cool enough to handle, remove and discard skins and chop coarsely. Meanwhile, toast pine nuts in now-empty skillet over medium heat, stirring often, until golden and fragrant, 4 to 5 minutes.

2 Place basil and parsley in 1-gallon zipper-lock bag. Pound bag with flat side of meat pounder or with rolling pin until all leaves are bruised.

3 Process garlic, pine nuts, and herbs in food processor until finely chopped, about 1 minute, scraping down sides of bowl as needed. With processor running, slowly add oil until incorporated. Transfer pesto to bowl, stir in Parmesan, and season with salt and pepper to taste. (Pesto can be refrigerated for up to 3 days or frozen for up to 3 months. To prevent browning, press plastic wrap flush to surface or top with thin layer of olive oil. Bring to room temperature before using.)

CREAMLESS CREAMY DRESSING

Makes about 2 cups

For an all-purpose dairy-free creamy dressing, we turned to cashews to achieve the perfect consistency. You'll need a conventional blender for this recipe; an immersion blender or food processor will produce dressing that is grainy and thin. Use raw unsalted cashews, not roasted, to ensure the proper flavor balance.

1	cup raw cashews
¾	cup water, plus extra as needed
3	tablespoons cider vinegar
1¼	teaspoons table salt
1	teaspoon onion powder
½	teaspoon sugar
¼	teaspoon garlic powder
2	tablespoons minced fresh chives
1	tablespoon minced fresh parsley
½	teaspoon pepper

1   Process cashews in blender on low speed to consistency of fine gravel mixed with sand, 10 to 15 seconds. Add water, vinegar, salt, onion powder, sugar, and garlic powder and process on low speed until combined, about 5 seconds. Let mixture sit for 15 minutes.

2   Process on low speed until all ingredients are well blended, about 1 minute. Scrape down blender jar. Process on high speed until dressing is smooth and creamy, 3 to 4 minutes. Transfer dressing to bowl. Cover and refrigerate until cold, about 45 minutes. Stir in chives, parsley, and pepper. Thin with extra water, adding 1 tablespoon at a time, to desired consistency. Season with salt and pepper to taste. (Dressing can be refrigerated for up to 1 week.)

CHIPOTLE-YOGURT SAUCE

Makes about 1 cup

Creamy yogurt makes for a simple sauce perfect for drizzling. This sauce is a great accompaniment to our Southwestern Shrimp and Oat Berry Bowl (page 122).

1	cup plain whole-milk yogurt
1	tablespoon minced canned chipotle chile in adobo sauce
1	teaspoon grated lime zest plus 2 tablespoons juice
1	garlic clove, minced

Whisk all ingredients together in bowl. Cover and refrigerate until flavors meld, at least 30 minutes. Season with salt and pepper to taste. (Sauce can be refrigerated for up to 4 days.)

Tahini-Yogurt Sauce

Omit chipotle and add ⅓ cup tahini. Substitute lemon zest and juice for lime.

Herb-Yogurt Sauce

Omit chipotle. Substitute lemon zest and juice for lime. Add 2 tablespoons minced fresh cilantro and 2 tablespoons minced fresh mint.

TOPPINGS AND SPRINKLES

The final touches to round out any bowl are the finishing toppings, whether you want to add a savory crunch, a textural contrast, or a last hit of added protein.

EVERYTHING BAGEL BLEND

Makes about ½ cup
This blend gives everything you sprinkle it on the aroma of everyone's favorite bagel and crunch.

2 tablespoons sesame seeds, toasted
2 tablespoons poppy seeds
1 tablespoon caraway seeds, toasted
1 tablespoon kosher salt
1 tablespoon dried minced onion
1 tablespoon dried minced garlic

Combine all ingredients in bowl. (Blend can be stored in airtight container for up to 3 months.)

SPICED PEPITAS OR SUNFLOWER SEEDS

Makes about ½ cup
Salty, crunchy, spicy seeds are an easy topping that elevates a basic bowl in a snap.

2 teaspoons extra-virgin olive oil or vegetable oil
½ cup raw pepitas or raw sunflower seeds
½ teaspoon paprika
½ teaspoon ground coriander
¼ teaspoon table salt

Heat oil in 12-inch skillet over medium heat until shimmering. Add pepitas, paprika, coriander, and salt. Cook, stirring constantly, until seeds are toasted, about 2 minutes; transfer to bowl and let cool. (Seeds can be stored in airtight container at room temperature for up to 5 days.)

CRISPY SHALLOTS

Makes about ½ cup
These are great for an oniony crunch. By using the microwave, there is minimal cleanup.

3 shallots, sliced thin
½ cup canola oil, for frying

Microwave shallots and oil in medium bowl for 5 minutes. Stir, then microwave for 2 more minutes. Repeat stirring and microwaving in 2-minute intervals until shallots are beginning to brown, then repeat stirring and microwaving in 30-second intervals until deep golden brown. Using slotted spoon, transfer shallots to paper towel–lined plate and season with salt to taste. Let drain and crisp for about 5 minutes. (Shallots can be stored in airtight container at room temperature for up to 1 month.)

QUICK-PICKLED VEGETABLES

Makes about 2 cups

This recipe works well with a single variety or a combination of vegetables such as onions, shallots, carrots, fennel, cabbage, and radishes. Trim and peel as needed. Halve and core fennel and cabbage before slicing. Shave carrots into ribbons for added contrast. Feel free to add up to 1 teaspoon of your favorite whole spices to the brine.

- 1   cup white or red wine vinegar
- ⅓   cup sugar
- ⅛   teaspoon table salt
- 2   cups thinly sliced hearty vegetables

Microwave vinegar, sugar, and salt in medium bowl until steaming, 2 to 3 minutes; whisk to dissolve sugar and salt. Add vegetables to hot brine and press to submerge completely. Let sit for 45 minutes. Drain. (Drained pickled vegetables can be refrigerated for up to 1 week.)

HARD- OR SOFT-COOKED EGGS

Serves 4

This recipe can be doubled; do not increase the water amount.

- 4   large eggs

Arrange trivet included with Instant Pot in base of insert and add 1 cup water. Using highest sauté function, bring water to boil. Set eggs on trivet. For hard-cooked eggs, lock lid into place and close pressure-release valve. Select high pressure-cook function and cook for 8 minutes. Turn off Instant Pot and quick-release pressure. Carefully remove lid, allowing steam to escape away from you. Using tongs, transfer eggs to bowl of ice water and let sit for 15 minutes. Peel before using. For soft-cooked eggs, follow directions above, but reduce pressure-cook time to 2½ minutes for fully set whites with runny yolks, or 3 minutes for fully set whites with fudgy yolks. Place eggs under cold running water for 30 seconds before peeling.

HOMEMADE YOGURT

Makes about 4 cups

The success of this recipe hinges on using yogurt that contains live and active cultures. The longer the yogurt cooks, the tangier it will be.

- 3½   cups whole milk
- ¼   cup plain yogurt with live and active cultures

1   Add milk to Instant Pot and, using highest sauté function, bring to 185 degrees. Turn off Instant Pot and strain milk through fine-mesh strainer into 8-cup liquid measuring cup. Let milk cool until it registers 110 degrees, stirring occasionally to prevent skin from forming, about 30 minutes.

2   Combine yogurt and ½ cup cooled milk in small bowl. Gently stir yogurt mixture into remaining cooled milk, then transfer to two 16-ounce Mason jars and seal; do not overtighten lids.

3   Place trivet included with Instant Pot in clean insert and add water until it reaches base of trivet. Place jars on trivet. Lock lid into place and open pressure-release valve. Select normal yogurt function and cook for 6 to 18 hours.

4   Turn off Instant Pot and carefully remove lid, allowing steam to escape away from you. Carefully remove jars and let yogurt cool at room temperature for 15 minutes. Transfer to refrigerator and let sit until fully chilled, about 3 hours. Stir yogurt to recombine before serving. (Yogurt can be refrigerated for up to 1 week; stir to recombine before serving.)

CHAPTER 1

CHICKEN

23 Chicken Noodle Soup with Shells, Tomatoes, and Zucchini

24 Chicken Harira

26 White Chicken Chili with Zucchini

28 Smoky Turkey Meatball Soup with Kale and Manchego

30 Chicken with Warm Bread and Arugula Salad

34 Chicken and Braised Radishes with Dukkah

36 Chicken and Barley Risotto with Butternut Squash and Kale

38 Chipotle Chicken and Black Beans with Pickled Cabbage

40 Javaher Polo with Chicken

44 Chicken with Spring Vegetables

46 Chicken with Spiced Whole Parsnips and Scallion-Mint Relish

49 Chicken and Potatoes with Fennel and Saffron

50 Soy Sauce Chicken with Gai Lan

52 Chicken and Couscous with Prunes and Olives

54 Chicken and Black Rice Bowl with Peanut-Sesame Dressing

57 Shredded Chicken Tacos with Mango Salsa

59 Chicken Sausages with White Beans and Spinach

60 Chicken in a Pot with Mashed Root Vegetables

Serves 6
Calories 480
Total Time 1¼ hours

CHICKEN NOODLE SOUP
WITH Shells, Tomatoes, and Zucchini

1 tablespoon canola oil

1 onion, chopped fine

1 tablespoon tomato paste

2 teaspoons minced fresh thyme or ½ teaspoon dried

8 cups water, divided

4 carrots, peeled, halved lengthwise, and cut into ½-inch pieces

2 celery ribs, halved lengthwise and cut into ½-inch pieces

2 tablespoons soy sauce

1 teaspoon table salt

1 (4-pound) whole chicken, giblets discarded

1 (8-ounce) zucchini, quartered lengthwise and sliced ¼ inch thick

2 tomatoes, cored and chopped

4 ounces (1 cup) 100 percent whole-wheat small pasta shells

¼ cup chopped fresh basil

WHY THIS RECIPE WORKS Chicken noodle soup is a perfect candidate for the Instant Pot because the high-heat pressure-cooking environment extracts tons of flavor and body-building gelatin from the meat, skin, and bones of a whole chicken. To keep the meat from overcooking while ensuring a deeply flavorful broth, it was crucial to get the timing exactly right. The Instant Pot heats from the bottom, so positioning the chicken breast side up exposed the dark meat thighs to more direct heat and shielded the delicate breast meat from overcooking. Once cooked, the tender meat was easy to shred and stir back in. We used the sauté function to simmer tomatoes and zucchini right in the broth toward the end of cooking so they could maintain their texture and flavor without getting blown out. Other small pasta shapes (whole wheat and traditional) can be substituted for the shells.

1   Using highest sauté function, heat oil in Instant Pot until shimmering. Add onion and cook until softened, 3 to 5 minutes. Stir in tomato paste and thyme and cook until fragrant, about 30 seconds. Stir in 6 cups water, scraping up browned bits, then stir in carrots, celery, soy sauce, and salt. Place chicken breast side up in pot.

2   Lock lid into place and close pressure-release valve. Select high pressure-cook function and cook for 20 minutes. Turn off Instant Pot and quick-release pressure. Carefully remove lid, allowing steam to escape away from you. Transfer chicken to carving board, let cool slightly, then shred into bite-size pieces using 2 forks; discard skin and bones.

3   Meanwhile, stir zucchini, tomatoes, shells, and remaining 2 cups water into soup and cook using highest sauté function until pasta is tender, about 8 minutes. Turn off Instant Pot. Return chicken and any accumulated juices to pot and let sit until heated through, about 2 minutes. Stir in basil and season with salt and pepper to taste. Serve.

CHICKEN HARIRA

2 (12-ounce) bone-in split chicken breasts, trimmed

1 tablespoon extra-virgin olive oil

1 tablespoon all-purpose flour

1 teaspoon grated fresh ginger

1 teaspoon ground cumin

½ teaspoon paprika

¼ teaspoon ground cinnamon

Pinch saffron threads, crumbled

10 cups chicken broth

1 cup dried brown or green lentils, picked over and rinsed

4 plum tomatoes, cored and cut into ¾-inch pieces

⅓ cup minced fresh cilantro

¼ cup Harissa (page 16), plus extra for serving

WHY THIS RECIPE WORKS For this nourishing meal, we put our spin on Moroccan harira, which is often used to break fast during Ramadan, as it is so filling and nutritious (made with lentils, tomatoes, fresh herbs, and often lamb). For our meat, bone-in split chicken breasts provided a flavorful lean protein; after browning them, we bloomed a fragrant combination of fresh ginger and warm spices. Flour provided some thickening power. Plum tomatoes stirred in at the end added traditional tomato flavor and freshness, while harissa gave us some heat and rounded out the depth of flavor. Large green or brown lentils work well in this recipe; do not use lentilles du puy (French green lentils). Store-bought harissa will also work well here.

1   Pat chicken dry with paper towels. Using highest sauté function, heat oil in Instant Pot until just smoking. Place chicken skin side down in pot and cook until well browned on first side, about 5 minutes; transfer to plate. Turn off Instant Pot.

2   Add flour, ginger, cumin, paprika, cinnamon, and saffron to fat left in pot and cook, stirring frequently, until fragrant, about 30 seconds. Slowly whisk in broth, scraping up any browned bits and smoothing out any lumps. Stir in lentils, then nestle chicken skin side up into lentil mixture and add any accumulated juices.

3   Lock lid into place and close pressure-release valve. Select high pressure-cook function and cook for 8 minutes. Turn off Instant Pot and quick-release pressure. Carefully remove lid, allowing steam to escape away from you. Transfer chicken to cutting board, let cool slightly, then shred into bite-size pieces using 2 forks; discard skin and bones.

4   Meanwhile, continue to cook lentils using highest sauté function until just tender, about 5 minutes. Turn off Instant Pot. Stir in chicken and any juices and tomatoes, and let sit until heated through, about 2 minutes. Stir in cilantro and harissa, and season with salt and pepper to taste. Serve, passing extra harissa separately.

Serves 6
Calories 340
Total Time 1 hour

WHITE CHICKEN CHILI WITH Zucchini

1½ tablespoons table salt
for brining

8 ounces (1¼ cups) dried
cannellini beans, picked
over and rinsed

2 poblano chiles,
stemmed, seeded,
and chopped coarse

1 onion, chopped coarse

2 jalapeño chiles, stemmed,
seeded, and chopped

1 tablespoon canola oil

1¼ teaspoons table salt

4 garlic cloves, minced

1 tablespoon ground cumin

2 teaspoons ground coriander

2 cups chicken broth

1½ pounds boneless, skinless
chicken thighs, trimmed

1½ cups fresh cilantro, trimmed
and cut into 2-inch lengths,
divided

2 zucchini (8 ounces each),
quartered lengthwise and
sliced ¼ inch thick

WHY THIS RECIPE WORKS What distinguishes a white chili from a red one is not its color, but rather the color of its ingredients—white poultry rather than beef or pork; white beans over red kidney beans; forgoing tomatoes; and green chiles instead of red ones. Using two peppers added a more complex flavor: Jalapeños gave a fresh, vegetal taste while poblanos brought a touch of earthiness. Lacking tomatoes and the fat and collagen of traditional beef stewing cuts, white chili can come out thin. To thicken our chili, we puréed just a portion of the white beans with some cilantro and then stirred this mixture back in to create a velvety, full-bodied texture that was vibrantly green, and creamy without any cream. By using boneless, skinless chicken thighs, we could cook dried cannellini beans at the same time without the beans blowing out or the chicken overcooking. Simmering zucchini in the stew after it cooked under pressure enabled the squash to keep its texture and turned the dish into a hearty meal. Serve with cubed avocado, lime wedges, and sour cream or Greek yogurt.

1 Dissolve 1½ tablespoons salt in 2 quarts cold water in large container. Add beans and soak at room temperature for at least 8 hours or up to 24 hours. Drain and rinse well.

2 Pulse poblanos, onion, and jalapeños in food processor until finely chopped, about 10 pulses, scraping down sides of bowl as needed. Transfer to bowl and set aside (do not wash food processor).

3 Using highest sauté function, heat oil in Instant Pot until shimmering. Add poblano mixture and salt and cook until mixture is softened and lightly browned, 5 to 7 minutes. Stir in garlic, cumin, and coriander and cook until fragrant, about 30 seconds. Stir in broth and beans, scraping up any browned bits, then nestle chicken into bean mixture. Lock lid into place and close pressure-release valve. Select high pressure-cook function and cook for 9 minutes.

4   Turn off Instant Pot and quick-release pressure. Carefully remove lid, allowing steam to escape away from you. Transfer chicken to cutting board, let cool slightly, then shred into bite-size pieces using 2 forks.

5   Meanwhile, transfer 1 cup cooked bean mixture and 1 cup cilantro to food processor and process until smooth, about 1 minute. Stir

zucchini into chili, partially cover, and cook, using highest sauté function, until just tender, about 4 minutes.

6   Stir in shredded chicken and any accumulated juices and processed bean mixture, and cook until heated through, about 1 minute. Top individual portions with remaining ½ cup cilantro and serve.

SMOKY TURKEY MEATBALL SOUP
WITH Kale and Manchego

1 slice hearty white sandwich bread, torn into quarters

¼ cup milk

1 ounce Manchego cheese, grated (½ cup), plus extra for serving

5 tablespoons minced fresh parsley, divided

½ teaspoon table salt

1½ pounds ground turkey

3 tablespoons extra-virgin olive oil, divided

1 onion, chopped

1 red bell pepper, stemmed, seeded, and cut into ¾-inch pieces

4 garlic cloves, minced

1 tablespoon smoked paprika

½ cup dry white wine

8 cups chicken broth

12 ounces kale, stemmed and chopped

WHY THIS RECIPE WORKS For this sunset-colored broth inspired by Spanish flavors, we started with a Spanish-style sofrito—a base of onion, bell pepper, and garlic—then added smoked paprika. After deglazing the pot with white wine, we poured in chicken broth, then dropped in the lean turkey meatballs (kept moist and tender thanks to a panade and Manchego, a sharp sheep's-milk cheese) and some chopped fresh kale. The soup required a mere 3 minutes under pressure, after which we brightened it with a sprinkling of fresh parsley and a touch of extra Manchego. Be sure to use ground turkey, not ground turkey breast (also labeled 99 percent fat-free), in this recipe.

1   Using fork, mash bread and milk into paste in large bowl. Stir in Manchego, 3 tablespoons parsley, and salt until combined. Add turkey and knead mixture with hands until well combined. Pinch off and roll mixture into 1-tablespoon-size balls.

2   Using highest sauté function, heat 1 tablespoon oil in Instant Pot until shimmering. Add onion and bell pepper and cook until softened and lightly browned, 5 to 7 minutes. Stir in garlic and paprika and cook until fragrant, about 30 seconds. Stir in wine, scraping up any browned bits, and cook until nearly evaporated, about 1 minute. Stir in broth and kale, then gently submerge meatballs in broth mixture.

3   Lock lid into place and close pressure-release valve. Select high pressure-cook function and cook for 3 minutes. Turn off Instant Pot and quick-release pressure. Carefully remove lid, allowing steam to escape away from you.

4   Stir in remaining 2 tablespoons parsley and remaining 2 tablespoons oil. Season with salt and pepper to taste. Serve, passing extra Manchego separately.

Serves 6
Calories 310
Total Time 1 hour

CHICKEN WITH WARM BREAD
AND Arugula Salad

2 (12-ounce) bone-in split chicken breasts, trimmed

¾ teaspoon table salt, divided

½ teaspoon pepper, divided

5 tablespoons extra-virgin olive oil, divided

3 (1-inch-thick) slices rustic white bread, cut into 1-inch pieces (4 cups)

½ cup water

2 sprigs fresh tarragon, plus 1 tablespoon minced

1½ tablespoons white wine vinegar

1 teaspoon Dijon mustard

½ fennel bulb, stalks discarded, bulb cored and sliced thin

3 scallions, sliced thin

3 tablespoons dried currants

5 ounces (5 cups) baby arugula

WHY THIS RECIPE WORKS This salad was heavily inspired by an offering created by the late renowned chef Judy Rodgers, from famed San Francisco restaurant Zuni Café. When she put her roast chicken with warm bread salad on the menu in the late '80s, it was a real hit. Now, a few decades later, it still is. The chicken was deeply bronzed, the meat juicy and well seasoned. The bread was tossed with savory chicken drippings. Currants, just-softened scallions and garlic, salad greens, and a sharp vinaigrette completed the salad. It was a perfect meal. But the recipe is anything but simple. It's a meticulously detailed four-page essay that could all be tackled easily in a professional kitchen, but at home it seemed taxing. We knew the Instant Pot was the ideal vessel to deliver this meal quickly, while keeping all cooking contained in one pot. Our tribute to the Zuni Café dish involved browning bone-in chicken breasts using the highest sauté function to render prized chicken fat, which we then used to lightly fry chunks of rustic bread directly in the pot. Next, we pressure-poached the chicken in tarragon water to infuse it with moisture and flavor. While the chicken cooked, we marinated currants, scallions, and fennel in a zippy, mustardy dressing that plumped the currants while softening and mellowing the fennel and scallions. For our third and final usage of the Instant Pot's versatility, the leftover chicken cooking liquid was simmered until it transformed into a concentrated essence, in which we tossed the toasted bread chunks to imbue them with masses of flavor while retaining their chicken-fat-fried crunch. The final dish was a bright, vinegary base with sweet hits of plump currants, warm chicken, and unforgettably crunchy cubes of toasted bread to add big hits of flavor without making the overall meal heavy.

Serves 4
Calories 530
Total Time 1 hour

If your chicken breasts are larger than 12 ounces, cut them in half crosswise before browning to ensure doneness.

1   Pat chicken dry with paper towels and sprinkle with ¼ teaspoon salt and ¼ teaspoon pepper. Using highest sauté function, heat 1 tablespoon oil in Instant Pot until just smoking. Place chicken skin side down in pot and cook until well browned on first side, about 5 minutes; transfer to plate.

2   Add 1 tablespoon oil and bread to fat left in pot and cook, using highest sauté function, stirring occasionally, until bread is crisp and browned, 10 to 12 minutes; transfer to bowl. Turn off Instant Pot. Add water and tarragon sprigs to now-empty pot, scraping up any browned bits. Place chicken skin side up in pot and add any accumulated juices. Lock lid into place and close pressure-release valve. Select high pressure-cook function and cook for 14 minutes.

3   Meanwhile, whisk vinegar, mustard, remaining ½ teaspoon salt, remaining ¼ teaspoon pepper, and remaining 3 tablespoons oil together in large bowl until smooth. Stir in fennel, scallions, currants, and minced tarragon; set aside.

4   Turn off Instant Pot and quick-release pressure. Carefully remove lid, allowing steam to escape away from you. Discard tarragon sprigs. Transfer chicken to cutting board and discard skin, if desired. Tent with aluminum foil and let rest while finishing salad.

5   Using highest sauté function, reduce cooking liquid to ⅓ cup, about 4 minutes. Add toasted bread and toss until liquid is absorbed. Add arugula to bowl with vinaigrette and toss to coat. Carve chicken from bones and slice ½ inch thick. Transfer salad to serving platter and top with chicken and croutons. Serve.

photo on following page >

Chicken with Warm Bread
and Arugula Salad, page 30

CHICKEN AND BRAISED RADISHES
WITH Dukkah

½ cup plain yogurt

¼ cup tahini

6 garlic cloves, minced, divided

4 teaspoons grated lemon zest, divided, plus 2 teaspoons juice

2 tablespoons minced fresh parsley

4 (6- to 8-ounce) boneless, skinless chicken breasts, trimmed

¾ teaspoon table salt, divided

¼ teaspoon pepper

4 teaspoons extra-virgin olive oil, divided

1½ pounds radishes, trimmed and halved lengthwise

½ cup chicken broth

3 tablespoons dukkah, divided

2 ounces (2 cups) watercress

WHY THIS RECIPE WORKS The Instant Pot is perfect for braising radishes because the quick time under pressure takes the bite out of them and turns them delicately sweet while maintaining their crunch. Submerging the radishes in a flavorful broth, we let them simmer until tender while the chicken, raised up out of the liquid, was able to cook. Dukkah, an Egyptian spice blend, added rich sweetness and warm spices, and we mixed a portion of it directly into the pot to amp up the flavor. While the chicken rested, we tossed the radishes with watercress, which balanced their now-sweet flavor. Warm radishes and chicken called for a cool, creamy sauce with a hint of acidity; a blend of nutty tahini, yogurt, lemon juice, and parsley was the perfect complement. The remaining dukkah, sprinkled on top, brought the whole dish together. If you can't find watercress, you can substitute baby arugula.

---

1   Combine yogurt, tahini, 1 teaspoon garlic, 1 teaspoon lemon zest, lemon juice, and parsley in small bowl and season with salt and pepper to taste; set aside for serving.

2   Cover chicken breasts with plastic wrap and pound thick ends gently with meat pounder until ¾ inch thick. Pat chicken dry with paper towels and sprinkle with ¼ teaspoon salt and pepper. Using highest sauté function, heat 1½ teaspoons oil in Instant Pot until just smoking. Add 2 pieces chicken smooth side down to pot and cook until well browned on first side, 3 to 5 minutes; transfer to plate. Repeat with 1½ teaspoons oil and remaining 2 pieces chicken; transfer to plate. Turn off Instant Pot.

3   Add remaining garlic and remaining 1 teaspoon oil to fat left in pot. Cook, using residual heat, stirring frequently, until fragrant, about 30 seconds. Stir in radishes, broth, 1 tablespoon dukkah, remaining 1 tablespoon lemon zest, and remaining ½ teaspoon salt, scraping up any browned bits. Arrange chicken browned side up in even layer on top of radishes and add any accumulated juices.

Serves 4
Calories 410
Total Time 1 hour

Lock lid into place and close pressure-release valve. Select high pressure-cook function and cook for 4 minutes.

4 Turn off Instant Pot and quick-release pressure. Carefully remove lid, allowing steam to escape away from you. Transfer chicken to cutting board, tent with aluminum foil, and let rest while finishing radishes.

5 Drain radishes in colander and transfer to large bowl. Add watercress to bowl, 1 handful at a time, and toss with warm radishes until watercress is slightly wilted, about 1 minute. Slice chicken ½ inch thick. Divide yogurt mixture among 4 individual serving plates and spread into even layer. Arrange radish mixture and chicken on top and sprinkle with remaining 2 tablespoons dukkah. Serve.

CHICKEN AND BARLEY RISOTTO
WITH Butternut Squash and Kale

2 (12-ounce) bone-in split chicken breasts, trimmed

½ teaspoon table salt, divided

¼ teaspoon pepper

1 tablespoon extra-virgin olive oil

4 cups butternut squash, cut into ½-inch pieces

1 onion, chopped fine

¾ cup pearl barley

1 teaspoon minced fresh thyme

½ cup dry white wine

1½ cups chicken broth, plus extra as needed

2 ounces blue cheese, crumbled (½ cup), plus extra for serving

5 ounces (5 cups) baby kale

WHY THIS RECIPE WORKS Pearl barley takes well to being cooked risotto-style; its starchy interior creates a velvety sauce when simmered, while maintaining a pleasant chewiness. Plus, it has more fiber and vitamins than traditional Arborio rice. The Instant Pot's concentrated, moist heat alleviates the need for constant monitoring typical of a risotto—creating a luxurious meal. To complement the hearty grain, we used the sauté function to soften onions and butternut squash before adding thyme, wine, and broth to the pot. Bone-in split chicken breasts, which we browned earlier, conveniently finished cooking atop the risotto. Placing the breasts on top of the barley allowed the chicken to render its juices into the risotto while still keeping the two components distinct. While the chicken breasts rested, we finished the risotto by stirring in baby kale for freshness and whisking in blue cheese for creamy richness. Do not substitute hulled, hull-less, quick-cooking, or presteamed barley (read the ingredient list on the package to determine this) in this recipe. If your chicken breasts are larger than 12 ounces, cut them in half crosswise before browning to ensure proper doneness.

1 Pat chicken dry with paper towels and sprinkle with ¼ teaspoon salt and pepper. Using highest sauté function, heat oil in Instant Pot until just smoking. Place chicken skin side down in pot and cook until well browned on first side, about 5 minutes; transfer to plate.

2 Add squash and onion to fat left in pot and cook, using highest sauté function, until onion is softened, 3 to 5 minutes. Stir in barley and thyme and cook until fragrant, about 1 minute. Stir in wine, scraping up any browned bits, and cook until nearly evaporated, about 1 minute.

Serves 4
Calories 570
Total Time 1 hour

3   Stir in broth and remaining ¼ teaspoon salt. Place chicken skin side up on top of squash mixture and add any accumulated juices. Lock lid into place and close pressure-release valve. Select high pressure-cook function and cook for 16 minutes.

4   Turn off Instant Pot and quick-release pressure. Carefully remove lid, allowing steam to escape away from you. Transfer chicken to cutting board and discard skin, if desired. Tent with aluminum foil and let rest while finishing risotto.

5   Add blue cheese to risotto and stir vigorously until risotto becomes creamy. Stir in kale, 1 handful at a time, until wilted, about 1 minute. Season with salt and pepper to taste, and adjust consistency with extra hot broth as needed. Carve chicken from bones and slice ½ inch thick. Transfer risotto to individual serving bowls, top with chicken, and sprinkle with extra blue cheese. Serve.

CHIPOTLE CHICKEN AND BLACK BEANS
WITH Pickled Cabbage

Pickled Cabbage

- ½ cup white wine vinegar
- 1 tablespoon sugar
- 1 teaspoon ground coriander
- 1½ cups shredded red cabbage

Chicken

- 4 (5- to 7-ounce) bone-in chicken thighs, trimmed
- 1 tablespoon canola oil
- 1 onion, chopped
- 4 teaspoons minced canned chipotle chile in adobo sauce, divided
- 3 garlic cloves, minced
- 1 teaspoon minced fresh oregano or ½ teaspoon dried
- ¾ cup chicken broth
- 2 (15-ounce) cans black beans, rinsed
- 1 cup fresh cilantro, trimmed and cut into 2-inch lengths, divided

WHY THIS RECIPE WORKS The Instant Pot's versatility makes it the one-stop-shop for almost every step of your dinner, from searing to sautéing, blooming to braising. First, we seared bone-in chicken thighs to render the chicken drippings so we could bloom smoky chipotle, garlic, and oregano in the flavorful fat. Then we cooked the chicken under pressure and created a magnificent broth. To sop up that deliciousness, we marinated canned black beans in the liquid as the chicken rested. On the side, we made a vinegar and coriander brine to quick-pickle red cabbage into a shockingly pink accompaniment. This sweet and sour bite offered a fresh, crunchy counter to the succulent chicken and spiced beans. The result was a hearty meal full of savoriness, heat, and piquancy. For a milder dish, omit the chipotle in step 6.

---

1 For the pickled cabbage Microwave vinegar, sugar, and coriander in medium bowl until steaming, 1 to 2 minutes; whisk to dissolve sugar. Add cabbage to hot brine and let sit, stirring occasionally, for 30 minutes. Drain cabbage and return to now-empty bowl; set aside for serving. (Pickled cabbage can be refrigerated for up to 3 days.)

2 For the chicken Meanwhile, pat chicken dry with paper towels. Using highest sauté function, heat oil in Instant Pot until just smoking. Place chicken skin side down in pot and cook until well browned on first side, about 5 minutes; transfer to plate.

3 Add onion to fat left in pot and cook, using lowest sauté function, until softened, 3 to 5 minutes. Stir in 1 tablespoon chipotle, garlic, and oregano and cook until fragrant, about 30 seconds. Stir in broth, scraping up any browned bits.

Serves 4
Calories 440
Total Time 1 hour

4 Place chicken skin side up in pot, adding any accumulated juices, and spoon some cooking liquid over top. Lock lid into place and close pressure-release valve. Select high pressure-cook function and cook for 9 minutes.

5 Turn off Instant Pot and quick-release pressure. Carefully remove lid, allowing steam to escape away from you. Transfer chicken to clean plate and discard skin, if desired. Tent with aluminum foil and let rest while finishing beans.

6 Stir beans and remaining 1 teaspoon chipotle into braising liquid and cook, using highest sauté function, until beans are heated through, about 2 minutes. Turn off Instant Pot. Stir in ¾ cup cilantro and season with salt and pepper to taste. Serve chicken with beans and pickled cabbage and top with remaining ¼ cup cilantro.

JAVAHER POLO WITH Chicken

½ cup plain yogurt

½ preserved lemon, pulp and white pith removed, rind rinsed and minced (2 tablespoons), plus 1 tablespoon brine

3 tablespoons chopped fresh cilantro, divided

1 teaspoon ground cardamom

1 teaspoon ground coriander

2 (12-ounce) bone-in split chicken breasts, trimmed and halved crosswise

¾ teaspoon table salt, divided

2 tablespoons canola oil, divided

1 onion, chopped fine

2 carrots, peeled and chopped fine

Pinch saffron threads, crumbled

2 cups chicken broth

1½ cups basmati rice, rinsed

¾ cup golden raisins, divided

½ cup slivered almonds, toasted, divided

½ cup pomegranate seeds, divided

WHY THIS RECIPE WORKS Javaher polo, a staple celebratory Persian dish of jeweled rice, is often served during wedding celebrations and special events, where its vibrant toppings are used to create intricate designs. Consisting of basmati rice perfumed with saffron and cardamom, the dish gets its name from the colorful dried fruit and nuts that traditionally stud its appealingly golden surface. We love the dish's subtle balance between sweet and savory, nuts and fruit, fresh and warm, and were inspired to create a recipe for the Instant Pot. By pairing the decorated rice with bone-in chicken breasts, we were able to create a delicately flavored and visually stunning complete dinner. To infuse umami flavor throughout, we browned the chicken breasts skin side down and then sautéed the onions and carrots in the rendered fat. We then pressure-cooked the rice and chicken with broth and saffron threads until the rice was tender and the chicken was cooked through. To finish, we chose golden raisins, toasted almonds, and pomegranate seeds for their discrete colors and flavors. For weeknight ease, we forewent the intricate design and opted instead to fold a portion of the toppings into the cooked rice and keep some out for a final garnish that created a pleasing textural contrast, with delicate flavor in every bite. A drizzle of lemony yogurt sauce elevated the meal with bright creaminess and pleasant tang.

Serves 4
Calories 760
Total Time 1 hour

You can substitute 1 tablespoon lemon zest for the minced preserved lemon, and fresh lemon juice for the preserved lemon brine. You can substitute long-grain white rice for the basmati rice.

1 Combine yogurt, preserved lemon brine, and 2 tablespoons cilantro in small bowl and season with salt and pepper to taste; set aside for serving.

2 Combine cardamom and coriander in separate small bowl. Pat chicken dry with paper towels and sprinkle with 1 teaspoon spice mixture and ¼ teaspoon salt. Using highest sauté function, heat 1 tablespoon oil in Instant Pot until just smoking. Place chicken skin side down in pot and cook until well browned on first side, about 5 minutes; transfer to plate.

3 Add onion, carrots, remaining 1 tablespoon oil, and remaining ½ teaspoon salt to fat left in pot and cook, using highest sauté function, until vegetables are softened, 3 to 5 minutes. Stir in remaining 1 teaspoon spice mixture and saffron and cook until fragrant, about 30 seconds. Stir in broth and rice, scraping up any browned bits. Nestle chicken skin side up into rice mixture and add any accumulated juices. Lock lid into place and close pressure-release valve. Select high pressure-cook function and cook for 7 minutes.

4 Turn off Instant Pot and quick-release pressure. Carefully remove lid, allowing steam to escape away from you. Transfer chicken to cutting board and discard skin, if desired. Tent with aluminum foil and let rest while finishing rice.

5 Sprinkle minced preserved lemon, ½ cup raisins, ¼ cup almonds, and ¼ cup pomegranate seeds over rice in pot. Lay clean dish towel over pot, replace lid, and let sit for 5 minutes. Fluff rice gently with fork to combine, then transfer to serving platter. Sprinkle rice attractively with remaining 1 tablespoon cilantro, remaining ¼ cup raisins, remaining ¼ cup almonds, and remaining ¼ cup pomegranate seeds. Serve chicken with rice and yogurt sauce.

photo on following page >

Javaher Polo with Chicken,
page 40

CHICKEN WITH Spring Vegetables

4 (5- to 7-ounce) bone-in chicken thighs, trimmed

¾ teaspoon table salt, divided

¼ teaspoon pepper

1 tablespoon extra-virgin olive oil, plus extra for drizzling

1 shallot, sliced thin

2 garlic cloves, sliced thin

Pinch red pepper flakes

2 cups chicken broth

1 pound small red potatoes, unpeeled, halved

3 sprigs fresh thyme

1 pound asparagus, trimmed and cut into 2-inch lengths

2 cups frozen peas

2 tablespoons chopped fresh tarragon

2 teaspoons grated orange zest

WHY THIS RECIPE WORKS For this recipe, we wanted to capture the vibrant flavors of springtime. Red potatoes, asparagus, and peas offered a variety of textures and flavors to accompany meaty chicken thighs. These items all cook at different rates, so we gave our chicken a head start by browning it before adding in garlic, shallot, and red pepper flakes. Then we added broth, red potatoes, and thyme, placed the chicken atop the potatoes, and cooked everything at once. Red potatoes have a higher moisture content than other potatoes, so they hold their shape under pressure. While the chicken rested, we stirred asparagus and peas into the pot. Simmering these vegetables only briefly kept them crisp-tender. Finally, licorice-y tarragon, fresh orange zest, and a drizzle of olive oil woke up the dish and rounded everything out. If using larger potatoes, cut them into 1½-inch pieces. Look for asparagus spears that are about ½ inch thick at the base.

---

1 Pat chicken dry with paper towels and sprinkle with ¼ teaspoon salt and pepper. Using highest sauté function, heat oil in Instant Pot until just smoking. Place chicken skin side down in pot and cook until well browned on first side, about 5 minutes; transfer to plate. Turn off Instant Pot.

2 Add shallot, garlic, and pepper flakes to fat left in pot and cook, using residual heat, until shallot is softened, about 1 minute. Stir in broth, potatoes, thyme sprigs, and remaining ½ teaspoon salt, scraping up any browned bits. Place chicken skin side up on top of potato mixture and add any accumulated juices. Lock lid into place and close pressure-release valve. Select high pressure-cook function and cook for 9 minutes.

3 Turn off Instant Pot and quick-release pressure. Carefully remove lid, allowing steam to escape away from you. Transfer chicken to serving platter and discard skin, if desired; tent with aluminum foil and let rest while finishing vegetables.

Serves 4
Calories 470
Total Time 1 hour

4 Discard thyme sprigs. Stir asparagus and peas into potato mixture, partially cover, and cook, using highest sauté function, until vegetables are crisp-tender, 3 to 5 minutes. Turn off Instant Pot.

5 Combine tarragon and orange zest in small bowl. Stir half of tarragon mixture into vegetables, and season with salt and pepper to taste. Serve chicken with vegetables, sprinkling individual portions with remaining tarragon mixture and drizzling with extra oil.

CHICKEN WITH SPICED WHOLE PARSNIPS AND Scallion-Mint Relish

¼ cup extra-virgin olive oil, divided

2 tablespoons white wine vinegar

1 tablespoon honey

1 teaspoon table salt, divided

4 scallions, sliced thin

4 (5- to 7-ounce) bone-in chicken thighs, trimmed

¼ teaspoon pepper

¾ teaspoon ground cardamom

¼ teaspoon ground cinnamon

⅛ teaspoon cayenne pepper

2 pounds parsnips, peeled, thin ends discarded

¾ cup chicken broth

¼ cup chopped fresh mint

¼ cup whole almonds, toasted and chopped

WHY THIS RECIPE WORKS Parsnips are rich in vitamins and minerals while being very low-calorie, so with the right cooking technique and a creative topping we knew they could really shine. While initial attempts at cooking small (and even medium) pieces of parsnips along with tender, juicy chicken thighs yielded mushy results, we ultimately achieved an ideal texture once we switched to using whole parsnips. Since root vegetables do an amazing job of absorbing the taste of whatever liquid they are cooked in, we knew we could add flavors such as cardamom, cayenne, and cinnamon by blooming them in the chicken fat rendered from the thighs before pressure-cooking the parsnips with chicken stock. The Instant Pot's concentrated heat created just the right environment to beautifully braise our whole parsnips and chicken thighs simultaneously; with just a dollop of a quick sweet and tangy scallion-mint relish, the dish was complete. Use parsnips that measure roughly 1½ inches in diameter at the thickest end; if necessary, larger parsnips can be halved lengthwise.

1   Whisk 3 tablespoons oil, vinegar, honey, and ¼ teaspoon salt together in medium bowl until honey has dissolved. Stir in scallions and set aside.

2   Pat chicken dry with paper towels and sprinkle with ¼ teaspoon salt and pepper. Using highest sauté function, heat remaining 1 tablespoon oil in Instant Pot until just smoking. Place chicken skin side down in pot and cook until well browned on first side, about 5 minutes; transfer to plate. Turn off Instant Pot.

3   Add cardamom, cinnamon, cayenne, and remaining ½ teaspoon salt to fat left in pot and cook, using residual heat, until fragrant, about 30 seconds. Add parsnips and toss to coat with spice mixture. Add broth, scraping up any browned bits, then arrange parsnips in even layer. Place chicken skin side up

Serves 4
Calories 620
Total Time 1 hour

on top of parsnips and add any accumulated juices. Lock lid into place and close pressure-release valve. Select high pressure-cook function and cook for 14 minutes.

4   Turn off Instant Pot and quick-release pressure. Carefully remove lid, allowing steam to escape away from you. Transfer chicken to serving platter and discard skin, if desired. Using large spoon, transfer parsnips gently to platter with chicken. Stir mint and almonds into scallion mixture and season with salt and pepper to taste. Dollop relish over chicken and parsnips. Serve.

Serves 4
Calories 480
Total Time 1 hour

CHICKEN AND POTATOES
WITH Fennel and Saffron

4 (5- to 7-ounce) bone-in chicken thighs, trimmed

¼ teaspoon pepper

2 tablespoons extra-virgin olive oil, divided

1 small fennel bulb, stalks discarded, bulb halved, cored, and sliced thin

4 garlic cloves, minced

1 tablespoon all-purpose flour

1 tablespoon tomato paste

¼ teaspoon saffron threads, crumbled

¼ cup Pernod

3 cups chicken broth, plus extra as needed

1 (14.5-ounce) can diced tomatoes, drained

1½ pounds Yukon Gold potatoes, unpeeled, cut into ¾-inch pieces

1 (3-inch) strip orange zest

1 tablespoon chopped fresh tarragon or parsley

WHY THIS RECIPE WORKS This bouillabaisse-inspired dinner exhibits the beauty of bold Provençal flavors, where taste isn't coming from butter or cream. The items that give bouillabaisse its robust flavor—garlic, fennel, and saffron—can withstand high pressure and made a fragrant broth, while browning the chicken and aromatics beforehand boosted savory flavor. A small amount of licorice-flavored liqueur provided the traditional anise note, while canned tomatoes lent brightness. We prefer to use Pernod in this recipe, but you can substitute other anise-flavored liqueurs. Do not use sambuca or Jägermeister. Serve with crusty bread.

1 Pat chicken dry with paper towels and sprinkle with pepper. Using highest sauté function, heat 1 tablespoon oil in Instant Pot until just smoking. Place chicken skin side down in pot and cook until well browned on first side, about 5 minutes; transfer to plate.

2 Add fennel to fat left in pot and cook, using lowest sauté function, until softened, 3 to 5 minutes. Stir in garlic, flour, tomato paste, and saffron and cook until fragrant, about 1 minute. Whisk in Pernod, scraping up any browned bits and smoothing out any lumps. Stir in broth, tomatoes, potatoes, and orange zest. Nestle chicken skin side up into potato mixture and add any accumulated juices.

3 Lock lid into place and close pressure-release valve. Select high pressure-cook function and cook for 9 minutes. Turn off Instant Pot and quick-release pressure. Carefully remove lid, allowing steam to escape away from you.

4 Transfer chicken to plate and discard skin, if desired. Discard orange zest. Adjust consistency of stew with extra hot broth as needed. Stir in tarragon and remaining 1 tablespoon oil; season with salt and pepper to taste. Transfer to individual serving bowls and top with chicken. Serve.

SOY SAUCE CHICKEN
WITH Gai Lan

¼ cup soy sauce

3 tablespoons Shaoxing wine or dry sherry

2 tablespoons packed brown sugar

5 garlic cloves, minced

1 tablespoon grated fresh ginger

½ teaspoon Sichuan chili powder

½ star anise pod

4 (5- to 7-ounce) bone-in chicken thighs, trimmed

1½ pounds gai lan, florets and leaves chopped, stalks cut into 3-inch lengths and halved lengthwise

3 scallions, sliced thin on bias

1 tablespoon toasted sesame oil

WHY THIS RECIPE WORKS For this mouthwatering chicken dish, we took inspiration from the beloved Chinese braise see yao gai, often found at Chinese BBQ restaurants. We created the superflavorful braising liquid with Shaoxing wine, soy sauce, star anise, and ginger. Pressure cooking for a mere 9 minutes trapped in all those sweet, salty, and spicy flavors to deeply infuse the chicken thighs. While the chicken rested, we stirred gai lan into the remaining liquid in the pot. Cooking the gai lan in stages allowed the long, slender stalks and small florets to stay crisp-tender, while the broad leaves wilted for a satisfying contrast. A sprinkle of scallions added a fresh finish, while a drizzle of toasted sesame oil added a nutty note. If you can't find Sichuan chili powder, you can substitute gochugaru. Another option is ½ teaspoon ancho chile powder plus a pinch of cayenne pepper. Quarter lengthwise gai lan stalks that are greater than 1 inch in diameter at the base. If you can't find gai lan, broccolini is a good substitute; separate stems and tops, and halve lengthwise any stems thicker than ½ inch in diameter at the base. Add ½ cup water to the pot with the broccolini stems, and increase the cooking time for the stems to 7 minutes.

---

1 Combine soy sauce, wine, sugar, garlic, ginger, chili powder, and star anise in Instant Pot. Add chicken, turn to coat, and arrange skin side down. Lock lid into place and close pressure-release valve. Select high pressure-cook function and cook for 9 minutes.

2 Turn off Instant Pot and quick-release pressure. Carefully remove lid, allowing steam to escape away from you. Transfer chicken to plate and discard skin, if desired. Tent with aluminum foil and let rest while preparing gai lan.

Serves 4
Calories 380
Total Time 45 minutes

3 Stir gai lan stems into cooking liquid, partially cover, and cook, using highest sauté function, until crisp-tender, about 3 minutes. Stir in gai lan leaves and florets, 1 handful at a time, and cook until bright green and wilted, 2 to 3 minutes.

4. Using slotted spoon, transfer gai lan to serving platter and top with chicken. Spoon some of remaining cooking liquid over top, sprinkle with scallions, and drizzle with oil. Serve.

CHICKEN AND COUSCOUS
WITH Prunes and Olives

4 shallots, sliced thin, divided (¾ cup)

1½ teaspoons red wine vinegar, divided

4 teaspoons extra-virgin olive oil, divided

4 (5- to 7-ounce) bone-in chicken thighs, trimmed

½ teaspoon table salt, divided

3 garlic cloves, minced

1 teaspoon dried oregano

¼ teaspoon red pepper flakes

1 cup chicken broth

¼ cup dry sherry

¾ cup chopped pitted prunes, divided

1½ cups boiling water

1 cup 100 percent whole-wheat couscous

⅓ cup pitted brine-cured green olives, halved

2 tablespoons capers, rinsed

1 cup fresh parsley leaves

WHY THIS RECIPE WORKS Chicken Marbella was created in the '80s at the Silver Palate food shop in New York City and was popularized by its cookbook. While we love the sugary, olive, prune, and caper base, we took it in a healthier direction to become a weeknight Instant Pot staple. The original version had all ingredients pulsed in a food processor and then marinated overnight. We eliminated this step and instead added the olives and capers after the chicken was cooked, enabling them to retain their brightness and individual textures (and sped up the overall process). Cooking some prunes under pressure turned them jammy and brought out their natural sugars to replace the hefty amount of brown sugar that we removed from the original recipe. We stirred the rest of the prunes directly into the couscous at the end, allowing their sweetness and texture to shine against the vinegar and sherry in this supertasty dish. If using traditional couscous, decrease boiling water to 1 cup.

---

1 Combine ¼ cup shallots, 1 teaspoon vinegar, and 1 teaspoon oil in small bowl; set aside. Pat chicken dry with paper towels and sprinkle with ¼ teaspoon salt. Using highest sauté function, heat remaining 1 tablespoon oil in Instant Pot until just smoking. Place chicken skin side down in pot and cook until well browned on first side, about 5 minutes; transfer to plate.

2 Add remaining shallots to fat left in pot and cook, using lowest sauté function, until shallots are softened, about 1 minute. Stir in garlic, oregano, and pepper flakes and cook until fragrant, about 30 seconds. Stir in broth, sherry, and ½ cup prunes, scraping up any browned bits. Place chicken skin side up in pot and add any accumulated juices. Lock lid into place and close pressure-release valve. Select high pressure-cook function and cook for 12 minutes.

Serves 4
Calories 520
Total Time 1 hour

3 Meanwhile, combine boiling water, couscous, and remaining ¼ teaspoon salt in large bowl. Cover and let sit for 10 minutes. Fluff couscous with fork and season with salt and pepper to taste; set aside.

4 Turn off Instant Pot and quick-release pressure. Carefully remove lid, allowing steam to escape away from you. Transfer chicken to serving platter and discard skin, if desired. Stir olives, capers, remaining ¼ cup prunes, and remaining ½ teaspoon vinegar into sauce, and season with salt and pepper to taste. Add parsley to shallot-vinegar mixture and toss to coat. Season with salt and pepper to taste. Serve chicken with couscous, sauce, and parsley salad.

CHICKEN AND BLACK RICE BOWL
WITH Peanut-Sesame Dressing

1½ pounds boneless, skinless chicken thighs, trimmed

1 tablespoon canola oil

1 (2-inch) piece ginger, peeled and sliced thin

1 lemongrass stalk, trimmed to bottom 6 inches and minced

2 cups water

1½ cups black rice, rinsed

½ teaspoon table salt

4 ounces sugar snap peas, strings removed, sliced thin on bias

2 carrots, peeled and cut into 2-inch-long matchsticks

2 ounces (1 cup) bean sprouts

1 recipe Peanut-Sesame Sauce (page 15)

½ cup fresh mint leaves, torn

WHY THIS RECIPE WORKS Black rice, loaded with antioxidants, was the perfect base for this nourishing and delicious bowl with Thai-inspired flavors. To infuse the rice with a piquant, citrusy taste, we started by blooming fresh ginger and lemongrass. To cook our chicken with the rice and prevent the dreaded over-cooking, we enclosed our thighs in a foil packet. This ensured moist meat while keeping the chicken from soaking up the dark purple color of the rice. For a variety of vegetables in our bowl we loved the sweetness of snap peas, the crunch of carrots, and the earthiness of bean sprouts. To finish, we drizzled the bowl with a savory peanut-sesame sauce. You can substitute an equal amount of long-grain brown rice for the black rice, if desired.

1 Arrange chicken in even layer in center of 20 by 12-inch sheet of aluminum foil. Bring short sides of foil together and crimp edges to seal tightly. Crimp open edges of packet.

2 Using highest sauté function, cook oil, ginger, and lemongrass in Instant Pot until fragrant, about 30 seconds. Stir in water, rice, and salt, scraping up any browned bits. Place foil packet on top of rice mixture. Lock lid into place and close pressure-release valve. Select high pressure-cook function and cook for 18 minutes.

3 Turn off Instant Pot and quick-release pressure. Carefully remove lid, allowing steam to escape away from you. Transfer foil packet to plate, brushing any rice back into pot. Discard ginger. Lay clean dish towel over pot, replace lid, and let sit for 5 minutes.

4 Meanwhile, carefully open foil packet and transfer chicken to cutting board; discard foil and any juices. Shred chicken into bite-size pieces using 2 forks. Fluff rice gently with fork. Transfer rice to individual serving bowls and top with chicken, snap peas, carrots, and bean sprouts. Drizzle with peanut-sesame sauce and sprinkle with mint. Serve.

Serves 4
Calories 600
Total Time 1 hour

Serves 4
Calories 560
Total Time 45 minutes

SHREDDED CHICKEN TACOS
WITH Mango Salsa

Salsa

- 1 ripe but firm mango, peeled, pitted, and cut into ¼-inch pieces
- ¼ cup fresh cilantro leaves
- 1 jalapeño chile, stemmed, seeded, and minced
- 1 small shallot, minced
- 1 tablespoon lime juice

Filling

- 1 tablespoon canola oil
- 4 garlic cloves, minced
- 1 teaspoon ground cumin
- ¼ teaspoon ground cinnamon
- 1 (8-ounce) can tomato sauce
- ½ cup chicken broth
- 2 tablespoons minced canned chipotle chile in adobo sauce plus 2 teaspoons adobo sauce
- ½ teaspoon table salt
- 1½ pounds boneless, skinless chicken thighs, trimmed and quartered

- 12 (6-inch) corn or flour tortillas, warmed
- 2 ounces cotija cheese, crumbled (½ cup)
- Lime wedges

WHY THIS RECIPE WORKS   For truly flavor-packed chicken tacos we bypassed boneless chicken breasts for boneless thighs, which are just as convenient but boast a meatier flavor. For a smoky taste, we used a substantial amount of chipotle peppers, cumin, and cinnamon, which also boosted the complexity of the sauce. We nestled the chicken into the sauce and relied on the moist heat of the Instant Pot to create saucy thighs that were meltingly tender in just 3 minutes. A potato masher allowed us to shred the chicken right in the pot, minimizing cleanup. Simmering the shredded chicken in the sauce before serving gave the sauce a chance to thicken and work its way into every crevice of the meat's abundant surface area. A sweet mango salsa was the refreshing foil to the smoky, meaty filling. A sprinkle of salty cotija was the final touch to kick taco night up a notch.

---

1   **For the salsa** Combine all ingredients in bowl and season with salt and pepper to taste; set aside for serving.

2   **For the filling** Using highest sauté function, cook oil, garlic, cumin, and cinnamon in Instant Pot until fragrant, about 3 minutes. Stir in tomato sauce, broth, chipotle and adobo sauce, and salt, scraping up any browned bits. Stir in chicken. Lock lid into place and close pressure-release valve. Select high pressure-cook function and cook for 3 minutes.

3   Turn off Instant Pot and quick-release pressure. Carefully remove lid, allowing steam to escape away from you. Using potato masher, mash chicken until coarsely shredded. Using highest sauté function, cook chicken until sauce has thickened, 5 to 7 minutes. Season with salt and pepper to taste. Serve chicken with tortillas, passing salsa, cotija, and lime wedges separately.

Serves 4 to 6
Calories 410
Total Time 45 minutes

CHICKEN SAUSAGES
WITH White Beans and Spinach

1 tablespoon extra-virgin olive oil, plus extra for drizzling

1½ pounds raw hot or sweet Italian chicken sausage

2 shallots, halved, and sliced thin

3 garlic cloves, minced

½ cup dry white wine

½ cup chicken broth

2 (15-ounce) cans cannellini beans, rinsed

12 ounces cherry tomatoes

1 sprig fresh rosemary

¼ teaspoon pepper

4 ounces (4 cups) baby spinach

2 ounces Parmesan cheese, shaved

WHY THIS RECIPE WORKS For this hearty braise, a simple combination of sausage, beans, and rosemary was transformed into a rich, warming ragout by the heat of the Instant Pot. We started with cannellini beans and Italian chicken sausage, which was full of spices (fennel and caraway) that provided ample flavor to the dish. We combined broth, wine, minced garlic, and rosemary for a flavorful liquid that seasoned the beans as they cooked. Once the sausages were cooked, we moved them to a platter to rest. Stirring some baby spinach into the beans before serving allowed it to wilt slightly—giving it a pleasing bite. Feel free to use any flavor of uncooked chicken sausage that you think will work well in this dish, or substitute turkey sausage. Any canned small white beans will work well here.

1   Using highest sauté function, heat oil in Instant Pot until just smoking. Add sausages and brown on all sides, 6 to 8 minutes; transfer to plate. Turn off Instant Pot.

2   Add shallots and garlic to fat left in pot and cook, using residual heat, until shallots are softened, about 1 minute. Stir in wine, scraping up any browned bits. Stir in broth, beans, tomatoes, rosemary sprig, and pepper. Nestle sausages into bean mixture and add any accumulated juices.

3   Lock lid into place and close pressure-release valve. Select high pressure-cook function and cook for 4 minutes. Turn off Instant Pot and quick-release pressure. Carefully remove lid, allowing steam to escape away from you.

4   Transfer sausages to plate and let rest while finishing beans. Discard rosemary sprig. Stir spinach into bean mixture, 1 handful at a time, until wilted, about 1 minute. Season with salt and pepper to taste. Transfer beans to serving platter and top with sausages. Sprinkle with Parmesan and drizzle with extra oil. Serve.

CHICKEN IN A POT
WITH Mashed Root Vegetables

1 (4-pound) whole chicken, giblets discarded

1¼ teaspoons table salt, divided

¾ teaspoon pepper, divided

1 tablespoon extra-virgin olive oil

2 teaspoons minced fresh rosemary

1 cup chicken broth

1 pound rutabaga, peeled and cut into 1-inch pieces

1 pound sweet potatoes, peeled and cut into 1-inch pieces

1 onion, peeled and quartered

¼ cup minced fresh chives

Lemon wedges

WHY THIS RECIPE WORKS This recipe makes it easy to cook both an entire chicken and our vegetable side of nutritious and low-in-calorie rutabaga and flavorful sweet potato simultaneously. We started by browning the chicken to create a deeper chicken savor. Adding the vegetables and broth directly into the pot allowed us to scrape up all the tasty chicken fond before locking the lid. Cooking the vegetables under the chicken enabled them to soak up the concentrated meat juices from the chicken, creating a buttery, sweet-savory mash. The chicken was done in a mere 24 minutes, and as it rested we strained the beautifully flavored jus, then mashed the vegetables right in the pot, sprinkling in fresh chives for an herbal-allium finish. A spritz of fresh lemon juice added a final burst of acidity to this flavor-packed, one-pot dinner. You can substitute parsnips for the rutabaga, if desired.

1   Pat chicken dry with paper towels and sprinkle with ¾ teaspoon salt and ½ teaspoon pepper. Tie legs together with kitchen twine and tuck wingtips behind back. Using highest sauté function, heat oil in Instant Pot until just smoking. Place chicken breast side down in pot and cook until well browned on first side, 6 to 8 minutes; transfer to plate. Turn off Instant Pot.

2   Add rosemary to fat left in pot and cook, using residual heat, until fragrant, about 30 seconds. Stir in broth, rutabaga, potatoes, onion, remaining ½ teaspoon salt, and remaining ¼ teaspoon pepper, scraping up any browned bits. Place chicken breast side up on top of vegetables and add any accumulated juices. Lock lid into place and close pressure-release valve. Select high pressure-cook function and cook for 24 minutes.

3   Turn off Instant Pot and quick-release pressure. Carefully remove lid, allowing steam to escape away from you. Transfer chicken to carving board, tent with aluminum foil, and let rest while preparing vegetables.

Serves 6
Calories 530
Total Time 1¼ hours

4. Strain broth and vegetables through fine-mesh strainer into fat separator. Return vegetables to now-empty pot and mash with potato masher until nearly smooth. Stir in chives and season with salt and pepper to taste. Let broth settle for 5 minutes, then transfer serving bowl and season with salt and pepper to taste. Carve chicken and discard skin, if desired. Serve chicken with vegetables, passing broth and lemon wedges separately.

CHAPTER 2

BEEF, PORK, AND LAMB

64   Double Vegetable Beef Stew with Lemon Zest

66   Hawaiian Oxtail Soup

70   Seared Flank Steak with White Bean and Sun-Dried Tomato Salad

72   Steak Tips with Warm Potato and Green Bean Salad

74   Braised Short Ribs with Daikon and Shiitakes

76   Boneless Short Ribs and Cauliflower Puttanesca

78   Shredded Beef Tacos with Jicama Slaw

81   Caldo Verde

82   Pork Pozole Rojo

84   Smothered Pork Chops with Leeks and Mustard

86   Pork and Bulgur Bowls with Parsley-Pepita Sauce

88   Creamy Parmesan Polenta with Eggplant, Sausage, and Tomatoes

90   Abgoosht

94   Lamb Meatballs with Creamy Lemon and Feta Orzo

DOUBLE VEGETABLE BEEF STEW
WITH Lemon Zest

1½ pounds boneless beef chuck-eye roast, trimmed and cut into 1½-inch pieces

1¼ teaspoons table salt, divided

2 tablespoons extra-virgin olive oil, divided

8 ounces cremini mushrooms, trimmed and halved if small or quartered if large

6 shallots, peeled and halved lengthwise

¼ cup all-purpose flour

1 tablespoon tomato paste

1 tablespoon minced fresh thyme or 1 teaspoon dried

¾ cup dry white wine

2 cups beef broth

1 pound small red or yellow potatoes, unpeeled, halved

12 ounces green beans, trimmed and cut into 1½-inch lengths on bias

3 carrots, peeled and sliced ¼ inch thick on bias

6 tablespoons chopped fresh parsley

1 tablespoon grated lemon zest

WHY THIS RECIPE WORKS For a healthier and faster beef stew, we turned to the Instant Pot and bulked up on vegetables to create a nourishing meal that kept its umami savor. After browning half of the meat (just enough for tasty fond without crowding the pot), we sautéed mushrooms and shallots before adding wine, broth, potatoes, and all the beef. Going under pressure for 25 minutes made the meat, potatoes, and shallots tender, and the stew rich and flavorful. Simmering a big helping of green beans and carrots at the end of cooking kept them vibrant and full of vegetal flavor. Lemon zest and minced parsley made for a refreshing finish. Boneless beef short ribs can be substituted for the chuck-eye roast. If using larger potatoes, cut them into 1½-inch pieces.

1 Pat beef dry with paper towels and sprinkle with ½ teaspoon salt. Using highest sauté function, heat 1 tablespoon oil in Instant Pot until just smoking. Brown half of beef on all sides, 5 to 7 minutes; transfer to bowl. Set aside remaining uncooked beef.

2 Add mushrooms, shallots, and remaining 1 tablespoon oil to fat left in pot and cook, using lowest sauté function, until mushrooms are softened, about 3 minutes. Stir in flour, tomato paste, and thyme and cook until fragrant, about 30 seconds. Stir in wine, scraping up any browned bits, and cook until mixture forms thick paste, about 30 seconds. Whisk in broth, smoothing out any lumps. Stir in potatoes and remaining ¾ teaspoon salt, then stir in browned beef and any accumulated juices and remaining uncooked beef.

3 Lock lid into place and close pressure-release valve. Select high pressure-cook function and cook for 25 minutes. Turn off Instant Pot and quick-release pressure. Carefully remove lid, allowing steam to escape away from you.

Serves 4 to 6
Calories 360
Total Time 1½ hours

4   Stir in green beans and carrots, partially cover, and cook, using lowest sauté function, until green beans and carrots are crisp-tender, 3 to 5 minutes. Combine parsley and lemon zest in bowl. Stir half of parsley mixture into stew and season with salt and pepper to taste. Sprinkle individual portions with remaining parsley mixture before serving.

HAWAIIAN OXTAIL SOUP

8 ounces fresh ginger, sliced thin, plus 4 table-spoons peeled and grated for serving

5 star anise pods

¼ ounce chen pi

3 pounds oxtails, fat trimmed to ¼ inch or less

8 cups water

½ cup raw peanuts

8 dried jujubes

1 ounce dried whole shiitake mushrooms, stemmed and rinsed

¼ cup soy sauce, plus extra as needed

½ teaspoon table salt

1 pound gai choy, trimmed and cut into 2-inch pieces

1 cup fresh cilantro leaves

4 scallions, sliced thin on bias

WHY THIS RECIPE WORKS Served anywhere from diners to bowling alleys, versions of this Hawaiian soup are venerated, with its tender meat, deeply perfumed broth, bountiful vegetables, and bright, fresh herbs. According to Leo Pascua, an avid home cook from O'ahu, people have strong opinions about their favorite one. He said, "Any self-respecting diner in Hawai'i will offer their version of oxtail soup. You defend the soup of your favorite diner and then go eat those of another diner to make sure you're right." Lynette Lo Tom, author of *A Chinese Kitchen: Traditional Recipes with an Island Twist*, explained that several distinct versions of oxtail soup in Hawai'i can be attributed to immigrant populations who brought their cooking traditions with them. The Chinese version of Hawaiian oxtail soup has a distinct profile—fresh ginger, star anise, and chen pi (aged dried mandarin orange peel)—and often contains peanuts, shiitakes, and jujubes. We set out to create an Instant Pot recipe that would deliver on traditional flavor, with the time-saving benefit of cooking under pressure. We started by testing how to extract the most balanced, beefy flavor from the oxtails. We found that, as long as we trimmed excess fat, tasters preferred tossing the oxtails into the pot without prior blanching or browning. To simplify straining the broth after cooking, we bundled the aromatics in cheesecloth. After just 1 hour under pressure (compared with the 4 hours required on the stovetop), we allowed the pot to release naturally for 30 minutes; this gradual drop in temperature and pressure gave the oxtail collagen more time to convert to silky gelatin. After transferring the solids to a platter, we strained the liquid through a fine-mesh strainer and skimmed excess fat from the surface to yield a clean, full-bodied broth. We returned the broth to the pot and added gai choy, and after 3 minutes of simmering, the peppery Chinese mustard green was crisp-tender and the broth steaming hot—ready to be ladled into deep bowls piled high with oxtails, tender shiitakes, and peanuts, and then topped with a tangle of cilantro and scallions. Finally, the dish would not have been complete without the added grated ginger and a splash of soy sauce.

Serves 4 to 6
Calories 520
Total Time 2¼ hours

Look for oxtails that are approximately 2 inches thick; thaw if frozen. If certain ingredients are difficult to find in a store or online, we suggest these substitutes, but the soup's flavor will be less nuanced as a result: You can substitute dry-roasted peanuts for the raw peanuts, 4 Medjool dates for the jujubes, 1½ tablespoons dried orange peel or 3 strips fresh orange zest for the chen pi, and 1 pound stemmed American mustard greens for the gai choy. Serve this soup in large, deep soup bowls. For a complete Hawaiian-style meal, serve with two scoops of white rice.

1   Bundle sliced ginger, star anise, and chen pi in single layer of cheesecloth and secure with kitchen twine. Add cheesecloth bundle, oxtails, water, peanuts, jujubes, mushrooms, soy sauce, and salt to Instant Pot.

2   Lock lid into place and close pressure-release valve. Select high pressure-cook function and cook for 60 minutes. Turn off Instant Pot and let pressure release naturally for 30 minutes. Quick-release any remaining pressure, then carefully remove lid, allowing steam to escape away from you.

3   Discard cheesecloth bundle. Using slotted spoon, transfer oxtails, peanuts, and mushrooms to large bowl, tent with aluminum foil, and let rest while finishing soup. Strain broth through fine-mesh strainer into separate large bowl or container, pressing on solids to extract as much liquid as possible; discard solids. Let broth settle for 5 minutes, then, using wide, shallow spoon or ladle, skim excess fat from surface. (Broth, oxtails, peanuts, and mushrooms can be refrigerated separately for up to 4 days. Reheat oxtails in simmering broth before adding gai choy in step 4.)

4   Return defatted broth to now-empty pot. Using highest sauté function, bring broth to simmer, then turn off Instant Pot. Stir in gai choy and cook, using residual heat, until wilted, about 3 minutes. Season with soy sauce to taste.

5   Thinly slice mushrooms, if desired. Divide oxtails, peanuts, and mushrooms among individual bowls, then ladle hot broth and greens over top. Sprinkle with cilantro and scallions. Serve, passing grated fresh ginger and extra soy sauce separately.

photo on following page >

Hawaiian Oxtail Soup,
page 66

SEARED FLANK STEAK
WITH White Bean and Sun-Dried Tomato Salad

3 tablespoons extra-virgin olive oil, divided

2 garlic cloves, sliced thin

1 (1-pound) flank steak, 1 inch thick, trimmed

¾ teaspoon table salt, divided, plus salt for cooking beans

½ teaspoon pepper, divided

2 (15-ounce) cans navy beans, rinsed

1 sprig fresh rosemary

1 bay leaf

2 tablespoons oil-packed sun-dried tomatoes, chopped coarse, plus 1 tablespoon tomato oil

2 tablespoons lemon juice

2 ounces (2 cups) baby arugula

¼ cup chopped fresh parsley

WHY THIS RECIPE WORKS A great flank steak can be beautifully seared in a hot skillet, and the Instant Pot's versatility easily replicates this with its highest sauté function. We started by crisping garlic directly in the pot and then using the garlicky oil to sear the steaks. The pressure function also came in handy while the steak rested, as it was the shortcut to a bean salad. For convenience we used canned beans, and although they can sometimes lack in taste, we infused their cooking liquid with rosemary and a bay leaf to saturate them with flavor. After the beans cooked under pressure for 1 minute, we tossed them with the crispy garlic, sun-dried tomatoes, peppery arugula, fresh parsley, and a zesty vinaigrette to serve alongside our exquisitely cooked steaks.

1   Using highest sauté function, heat 2 tablespoons olive oil in Instant Pot until shimmering. Add garlic and cook, stirring often, until beginning to brown, 2 to 3 minutes. Turn off Instant Pot and continue to cook, using residual heat, until garlic is evenly golden brown and crisp, 2 to 3 minutes. Using slotted spoon, transfer garlic to paper towel–lined plate; set aside.

2   Cut steak in half lengthwise, then cut each piece in half crosswise to create 4 steaks. Pat steaks dry with paper towels and sprinkle with ¼ teaspoon salt and ¼ teaspoon pepper. Using highest sauté function, heat oil left in pot until just smoking. Add steaks and cook until well browned and meat registers 120 to 125 degrees (for medium-rare) or 130 to 135 degrees (for medium), 3 to 7 minutes per side. Turn off Instant Pot and transfer steaks to cutting board, tent with aluminum foil, and let rest while preparing beans.

Serves 4
Calories 490
Total Time 45 minutes

3 Add beans, 2 cups water, ½ teaspoon salt, rosemary sprig, and bay leaf to now-empty pot. Lock lid into place and close pressure-release valve. Select high pressure-cook function and cook for 1 minute. Turn off Instant Pot and quick-release pressure. Carefully remove lid, allowing steam to escape away from you. Drain beans; discard rosemary sprig and bay leaf.

4 Whisk tomato oil, lemon juice, remaining 1 tablespoon olive oil, remaining ½ teaspoon salt, and remaining ¼ teaspoon pepper together in large bowl. Add beans, arugula, parsley, tomatoes, and garlic and toss to combine. Season with salt and pepper to taste. Slice steaks thin against grain and serve with salad.

STEAK TIPS
WITH Warm Potato and Green Bean Salad

1½ pounds small red potatoes, unpeeled, halved

2 (2-inch) strips lemon zest plus 1 tablespoon juice

¾ teaspoon table salt, divided, plus salt for cooking potatoes

8 ounces green beans, trimmed and cut on bias into 1-inch lengths

1 pound sirloin steak tips, trimmed and cut into 2-inch pieces

¼ teaspoon pepper

1 tablespoon extra-virgin olive oil

¼ cup plain yogurt

¼ cup chopped fresh parsley

1 shallot, minced

2 tablespoons mayonnaise

1 tablespoon whole-grain mustard

2 teaspoons capers, rinsed and minced

WHY THIS RECIPE WORKS Steak tips don't need much more than a good sear in a hot skillet, so we opted to use the Instant Pot's highest sauté function to cook the steak and then used the pressure function to fast-track a delicious side dish: warm potato and green bean salad with a tangy dressing. In just a few minutes under pressure, our potatoes (flavored with lemon zest) were tender and ready to be finished, while the hearty helping of green beans just needed a brief simmer to warm and soften slightly. In the time it took the drained veggies to cool slightly, we browned our steak tips to a perfect medium-rare. To finish, we dressed the still-warm potatoes and bright green beans in a flavor-packed dressing. For a lower-fat potato salad, we subbed yogurt for some of the traditional mayo and mixed it with whole-grain mustard, shallots, parsley, and capers. Use potatoes measuring 1 to 2 inches in diameter; if using larger potatoes cut them into 1½-inch pieces. Sirloin steak tips, also known as flap meat, can be sold as whole steaks, cubes, and strips; we prefer to purchase whole steaks and cut them ourselves.

1   Add potatoes, 4 cups water, lemon zest, and ½ teaspoon salt to Instant Pot. Lock lid into place and close pressure-release valve. Select high pressure-cook function and cook for 3 minutes. Turn off Instant Pot and quick-release pressure. Carefully remove lid, allowing steam to escape away from you.

2   Stir green beans into pot with potatoes, partially cover, and cook, using highest sauté function, until beans are crisp-tender, 3 to 5 minutes. Drain potatoes and green beans; discard lemon zest. Let vegetables cool while preparing steak tips.

Serves 4
Calories 430
Total Time 1 hour

3 Pat steak tips dry with paper towels and sprinkle with ¼ teaspoon salt and pepper. Using highest sauté function, heat oil in clean, dry Instant Pot until just smoking. Add steak tips and cook until well browned on all sides and meat registers 120 to 125 degrees (for medium-rare) or 130 to 135 degrees (for medium), 6 to 8 minutes.

4 Whisk yogurt, parsley, shallot, mayonnaise, mustard, lemon juice, capers, and remaining ½ teaspoon salt together in large bowl. Add vegetables to bowl with dressing and toss gently to combine. Season with salt and pepper to taste. Serve steak tips with salad.

BRAISED SHORT RIBS
WITH Daikon and Shiitakes

6 scallions, white and green parts separated and cut into 1-inch pieces

6 garlic cloves, lightly crushed and peeled

1 (1-inch) piece ginger, sliced thin

1 tablespoon canola oil

1 cup sake or dry white wine

1 cup water

1 Asian pear, halved, cored, and cut into 1-inch pieces

1 ounce dried shiitake mushrooms, stemmed and rinsed

3 tablespoons soy sauce

2 tablespoons sugar

1 tablespoon unseasoned rice vinegar

1 pound boneless beef short ribs, trimmed and cut into 1½-inch pieces

1½ pounds daikon radishes, peeled and cut into 1-inch pieces

1 cup peeled cooked chestnuts, broken into large pieces (optional)

8 dried jujubes, pitted and halved

WHY THIS RECIPE WORKS Galbi-jjim (braised short ribs) is considered a special-occasion dish in Korea and is a delicious and nutritious Instant Pot classic. In this version, we sautéed the aromatics—scallions, garlic, and ginger—which proved crucial for building flavor. We did not brown the ribs but braised them, along with an Asian pear (for fruity sweetness) and a generous handful of earthy shiitake mushrooms, directly in an aromatic liquid seasoned with sake, soy sauce, and rice vinegar. We kept the protein amount moderate while loading up on daikon radishes to make the meal filling and hearty. The radishes also worked to balance the rich sweetness of the dish, so we stirred them in toward the end of cooking to keep their crunchy freshness. To finish the dish, we simmered sweet jujubes and nutty chestnuts alongside the radishes to add some final indulgent flavor. Defatting the cooking liquid ensured that the sauce was rich but not greasy, while knocking flavor out of the park. You can substitute boneless beef chuck-eye roast for the short ribs. If jujubes are unavailable, substitute 6 Medjool dates.

1   Using highest sauté function, cook scallion whites, garlic, ginger, and oil in Instant Pot until fragrant, about 2 minutes. Stir in sake and cook until reduced by half, about 2 minutes.

2   Stir in water, pear, mushrooms, soy sauce, sugar, and vinegar. Nestle short ribs into pot. Lock lid into place and close pressure-release valve. Select high pressure-cook function and cook for 40 minutes.

3   Turn off Instant Pot and quick-release pressure. Carefully remove lid, allowing steam to escape away from you. Using slotted spoon, transfer beef and mushrooms to serving platter, tent with aluminum foil, and let rest while finishing sauce.

Serves 4
Calories 500
Total Time 2 hours

4 Strain braising liquid through fine-mesh strainer into fat separator; discard solids. Let braising liquid settle for 5 minutes, then return defatted liquid to now-empty pot. Stir in radishes, chestnuts, if using, and jujubes. Partially cover pot and cook, using highest sauté function, until radishes are tender and jujubes are plump, 3 to 5 minutes.

5 Quarter mushrooms, if desired. Divide short ribs and mushrooms evenly among serving bowls. Ladle sauce, radishes, chestnuts, and jujubes evenly over short ribs and mushrooms. Sprinkle with scallion greens. Serve.

BONELESS SHORT RIBS
AND Cauliflower Puttanesca

1 pound boneless beef short ribs, trimmed and cut into 1½-inch pieces

¼ teaspoon table salt

¼ teaspoon pepper

1 tablespoon extra-virgin olive oil

5 garlic cloves, minced

4 anchovy fillets, minced

1 tablespoon tomato paste

¼ teaspoon red pepper flakes

1 (28-ounce) can whole peeled tomatoes, drained with ½ cup juice reserved, halved

1½ pounds cauliflower florets, cut into 1½-inch pieces

¼ cup pitted brine-cured black olives, chopped coarse

¼ cup minced fresh parsley

2 tablespoons capers, rinsed

WHY THIS RECIPE WORKS Pressure cooking can blow out light aromatics, so starting with bold ingredients is a great way to develop balanced flavor as they mellow in the pot. Therefore, the strong flavors of a classic puttanesca sauce—anchovies, garlic, capers, olives, and tomatoes—were a great fit for the 40 minutes needed to render boneless short ribs meltingly tender (a fraction of the time it traditionally takes). Instead of starchy pasta, we turned to nutrient-rich cauliflower for a filling side. Its mild flavor absorbed the braising liquid beautifully and added tasty bulk without many calories or carbs. Stirring everything together and drizzling it with olive oil brought this deceptively rich (while shockingly healthy) dish to life. Look for lean ribs cut from the chuck that are 1½ to 2 inches thick. You can substitute boneless beef chuck-eye roast for the short ribs.

***

1 Pat short ribs dry with paper towels and sprinkle with salt and pepper. Using highest sauté function, heat oil in Instant Pot until just smoking. Add short ribs and brown on all sides, 6 to 8 minutes; transfer to plate. Turn off Instant Pot.

2 Add garlic, anchovies, tomato paste, and pepper flakes to fat left in pot. Cook, stirring frequently, using residual heat, until fragrant, about 30 seconds. Stir in tomatoes and reserved juice, scraping up any browned bits. Nestle short ribs into tomato mixture and add any accumulated juices. Lock lid into place and close pressure-release valve. Select high pressure-cook function and cook for 40 minutes.

3 Turn off Instant Pot and quick-release pressure. Carefully remove lid, allowing steam to escape away from you. Transfer beef to plate, tent with aluminum foil, and let rest while finishing cauliflower and sauce.

Serves 4
Calories 340
Total Time 1½ hours

4 Strain braising liquid through fine-mesh strainer into fat separator; transfer solids to now-empty pot. Let braising liquid settle for 5 minutes, then pour defatted liquid into pot with solids. Stir in cauliflower and bring to simmer using highest sauté function. Partially cover and cook, stirring occasionally, until cauliflower is tender, 4 to 6 minutes. Turn off Instant Pot.

5 Gently stir in beef and any accumulated juices, olives, parsley, and capers. Partially cover and let sit until heated through, about 2 minutes. Season with salt and pepper to taste. Serve.

SHREDDED BEEF TACOS
WITH Jicama Slaw

Filling

3 tablespoons ancho chile powder

3 tablespoons tomato paste

2 tablespoons vegetable oil

3 garlic cloves, minced

2 teaspoons ground cumin

2 teaspoons dried oregano

¼ teaspoon ground cloves

½ teaspoon table salt

1 cup full-bodied lager

1½ pounds boneless beef chuck-eye roast, trimmed and cut into 1-inch pieces

Jicama Slaw

1 cup distilled white vinegar

2 tablespoons sugar

6 radishes, trimmed and sliced thin

1 carrot, peeled and shredded

12 ounces jicama, peeled and cut into 2-inch-long matchsticks

¼ cup fresh cilantro leaves

12 (6-inch) corn or flour tortillas, warmed

WHY THIS RECIPE WORKS Chuck roast, with its big beefy flavor, is the ideal basis for taco filling because it becomes meltingly tender and shreddable in the Instant Pot, plus it is inexpensive and easy to find. Cutting the roast into 1-inch pieces helped it cook faster and, as a result, become even more tender than when left whole. To make our well-spiced sauce we combined a flavorful mixture of dried ancho chiles, tomato paste, garlic, cumin, oregano, and a hint of clove; blooming these aromatics with oil in the pressure cooker brought out their full flavor. We then added our beef pieces and some beer to the pot and cooked everything for half an hour to soften and infuse the beef with flavor. To complement the warm spices of the beef, we created a cool and tangy jicama, radish, and carrot slaw, which we quickly brined while the beef cooked. Once the beef was pull-apart tender, we simply mashed it in the pot and simmered it briefly to the desired consistency. Boneless beef short ribs can be substituted for the chuck-eye roast. If jicama is unavailable, double the amount of radishes and carrot in the slaw.

1 **For the filling** Combine ancho chile powder, tomato paste, oil, garlic, cumin, oregano, cloves, and salt in Instant Pot. Using highest sauté function, cook, stirring frequently, until fragrant, about 3 minutes. Whisk in beer, scraping up any browned bits and smoothing out any lumps. Stir in beef until evenly coated in spice mixture. Lock lid into place and close pressure-release valve. Select high pressure-cook function and cook for 30 minutes.

2 **For the jicama slaw** Meanwhile, microwave vinegar and sugar in medium bowl until steaming, 2 to 3 minutes; whisk to dissolve sugar. Add radishes and carrot to hot brine and let sit, stirring occasionally, for 30 minutes. Measure out and reserve 1 tablespoon brine, then drain vegetables and return to now-empty bowl. Add reserved brine and jicama and toss to combine; set aside. (Slaw can be refrigerated for up to 24 hours.)

Serves 4 to 6
Calories 400
Total Time 1 hour

3 Turn off Instant Pot and quick-release pressure. Carefully remove lid, allowing steam to escape away from you. Skim excess fat from top of filling using wide, shallow spoon. Using potato masher, smash beef until coarsely shredded.

Using highest sauté function, cook filling until sauce has thickened, about 5 minutes. Season with salt and pepper to taste.

4 Stir cilantro into slaw. Serve beef with tortillas and slaw.

CALDO VERDE

¼ cup extra-virgin olive oil, divided

12 ounces Portuguese chouriço or linguiça sausage, cut into ½-inch pieces

1 onion, chopped fine

4 garlic cloves, minced

¼ teaspoon red pepper flakes

4 cups chicken broth

4 cups water

2 pounds Yukon Gold potatoes, peeled and cut into ¾-inch pieces

1 pound collard greens, stemmed and cut into 1-inch pieces

2 teaspoons white wine vinegar

WHY THIS RECIPE WORKS Everything about caldo verde, the classic Portuguese soup of smoky sausage, potatoes, and sturdy greens, is hearty and satisfying. Its intentionally thin broth is usually made with just water, but for our version we wanted something with a little more body (and a few more nutrients), so we settled on a 50/50 ratio of water and chicken broth. Using plenty of potatoes, a pound of collard greens, and savory chouriço turned this simple soup into a filling meal. We chose Yukon Golds because they held their shape better than russets. If Portuguese chouriço or linguiça sausage is unavailable, Spanish semicured chorizo can be substituted. We prefer collard greens here for their delicate sweetness and meatier bite, but kale can be substituted. Serve with hearty bread.

---

1 Using highest sauté function, heat 1 tablespoon oil in Instant Pot until shimmering. Add chouriço and cook until rendered and beginning to brown, about 5 minutes. Stir in onion and cook until softened, about 5 minutes. Stir in garlic and pepper flakes and cook until fragrant, about 30 seconds.

2 Stir in broth and water, scraping up any browned bits, then stir in potatoes and collard greens. Lock lid into place and close pressure-release valve. Select high pressure-cook function and cook for 8 minutes.

3 Turn off Instant Pot and quick-release pressure. Carefully remove lid, allowing steam to escape away from you. Stir in vinegar and remaining 3 tablespoons oil. Season with salt and pepper to taste. Serve.

PORK POZOLE ROJO

8 ounces (1¼ cups) dried whole white or yellow hominy

1 tablespoon extra-virgin olive oil

1 onion, chopped fine

2 tablespoons ancho chile powder

5 garlic cloves, minced

1 teaspoon dried oregano

4 cups chicken broth

1½ pounds boneless country-style pork ribs, trimmed and cut into 1-inch pieces

1 teaspoon table salt

½ teaspoon pepper

2 bay leaves

WHY THIS RECIPE WORKS This wholesome Mexican soup of pork, hominy, and alliums is infinitely customizable and a great option for pressure cooking. To achieve richness and depth, we skipped browning the pork and focused instead on building an intense base by softening onion and blooming ancho chile powder, garlic, and oregano for flavorful fond in the pot. Country-style pork ribs turned soft and juicy under pressure and were a leaner, more convenient choice than boneless pork butt. Hominy is essential to pozole, and we found that dried hominy, which we soaked, cooked through properly with the pork, and the starches it released under pressure gave the soup extra body. You can substitute two (15-ounce) cans rinsed hominy. Boneless pork butt can be substituted for the ribs. We like to serve our pozole with shredded cabbage, thinly sliced radishes, diced avocado, cilantro, lime wedges, and a little extra oregano.

1 Place hominy and 2 quarts cold water in large container. Let soak at room temperature for at least 8 hours or up to 24 hours. Drain and rinse well.

2 Using highest sauté function, heat oil in Instant Pot until shimmering. Add onion and cook until softened and lightly browned, 5 to 7 minutes. Add ancho chile powder, garlic, and oregano and cook, stirring frequently, until fragrant, about 30 seconds. Stir in broth, scraping up any browned bits. Stir in pork, hominy, salt, pepper, and bay leaves.

3 Lock lid into place and close pressure-release valve. Select high pressure-cook function and cook for 25 minutes. Turn off Instant Pot and quick-release pressure. Carefully remove lid, allowing steam to escape away from you.

4 Discard bay leaves. Using wide, shallow spoon, skim excess fat from surface of soup. Season with salt and pepper to taste. Serve.

Serves 4 to 6
Calories 400
Total Time 1 hour, plus
8 hours soaking

SMOTHERED PORK CHOPS
WITH Leeks and Mustard

4 (8- to 10-ounce) bone-in blade-cut pork chops, ¾ inch thick, trimmed

½ teaspoon table salt

½ teaspoon pepper

4 teaspoons extra-virgin olive oil, divided

2 ounces pancetta, chopped fine

1 tablespoon all-purpose flour

¾ cup dry white wine

1½ pounds leeks, ends trimmed, halved lengthwise, sliced into 3-inch lengths, and washed thoroughly

1 tablespoon Dijon mustard

2 tablespoons chopped fresh parsley

WHY THIS RECIPE WORKS This French take on smothered pork chops uses the Instant Pot to transform a hefty pound and a half of leeks (including their usually tough dark green parts) into a luscious, pungent, meltingly tender topping for our flavorful pork chops. Blade chops have a combination of light and dark meat, connective tissue, marbled fat, and bone, which makes them ideal for pressure cooking, as the meat becomes tender and moist. After browning the pork chops directly in the pot, we set them aside to cook salty pancetta before adding wine, leeks, and a little flour to make a rich, savory gravy infused with meaty flavor. We added the browned chops back in and cooked the whole thing under pressure until the pork was tender and the leeks had cooked down to a rich consistency. Taking a cue from classic French flavors, we combined the sweet, aromatic leeks with tangy Dijon mustard. Bacon can be substituted for the pancetta.

1   Using sharp knife, cut 2 slits, about 2 inches apart, through fat on edge of each pork chop. Pat chops dry with paper towels and sprinkle with salt and pepper. Using highest sauté function, heat 2 teaspoons oil in Instant Pot until just smoking. Brown 2 chops on both sides, 6 to 8 minutes; transfer to plate. Repeat with remaining 2 teaspoons oil and remaining chops; transfer to plate.

2   Add pancetta to fat left in pot and cook, using highest sauté function, until softened and lightly browned, about 2 minutes. Stir in flour and cook for 30 seconds. Stir in wine, scraping up any browned bits and smoothing out any lumps. Stir in leeks and cook until softened, about 3 minutes. Nestle pork chops into pot (chops will overlap) and add any accumulated juices. Lock lid into place and close pressure-release valve. Select high pressure-cook function and cook for 10 minutes.

Serves 4
Calories 550
Total Time 1½ hours

3 Turn off Instant Pot and let pressure release naturally for 15 minutes. Quick-release any remaining pressure, then carefully remove lid, allowing steam to escape away from you. Transfer pork chops to serving platter, tent with aluminum foil, and let rest while finishing leeks.

4 Using highest sauté function, bring leek mixture to simmer. Stir in mustard and cook until slightly thickened, about 5 minutes. Season with salt and pepper to taste. Spoon leek mixture over pork chops and sprinkle with parsley. Serve.

PORK AND BULGUR BOWLS
WITH Parsley-Pepita Sauce

5 tablespoons extra-virgin olive oil, divided

3 garlic cloves, minced, divided

2 teaspoons dried oregano, divided

¼ cup dry white wine

1½ cups chicken broth, plus extra as needed

1 teaspoon table salt, divided

1 pound boneless country-style pork ribs, trimmed and cut into 1½-inch pieces

¾ cup minced fresh parsley

¼ cup roasted, unsalted pepitas

¼ teaspoon red pepper flakes

1½ cups medium-grind bulgur

1 recipe Quick-Pickled Carrots (page 19)

WHY THIS RECIPE WORKS Creating the components of a grain bowl in the Instant Pot is all about timing and maximizing your ingredients. We built a flavorful braising liquid for our pork ribs that doubled as the bulgur cooking liquid. Bulgur was ideal for healthy Instant Pot cooking, as it is full of vitamins and fiber, plus it needed only 3 minutes to cook while the ribs rested. We arranged the pork over the bulgur and topped everything with a vibrant sauce made of parsley, pepitas, garlic, and a generous amount of extra-virgin olive oil. We finished our bowl with some tangy quick-pickled carrots. Boneless pork butt can be substituted for the ribs. Do not use cracked wheat; it has a longer cook time and will not work in this recipe.

1   Using highest sauté function, cook 1 tablespoon oil, two-thirds garlic, and 1 teaspoon oregano in Instant pot, stirring frequently, until fragrant, about 3 minutes. Stir in wine, broth, and ½ teaspoon salt, scraping up any browned bits, then stir in pork. Lock lid into place and close pressure-release valve. Select high pressure-cook function and cook for 25 minutes.

2   Meanwhile, combine parsley, pepitas, pepper flakes, remaining ¼ cup oil, remaining garlic, and remaining 1 teaspoon oregano in bowl. Season with salt and pepper to taste, and set aside for serving.

3   Turn off Instant Pot and quick-release pressure. Carefully remove lid, allowing steam to escape away from you. Using slotted spoon, transfer pork to serving platter, tent with aluminum foil, and let rest while cooking bulgur. Strain braising liquid through fine-mesh strainer into 4-cup liquid measuring cup; discard solids. Using wide, shallow spoon, skim excess fat from surface. Add extra broth as needed to equal 2½ cups.

Serves 4
Calories 550
Total Time 1½ hours

4 Combine braising liquid, bulgur, and remaining ½ teaspoon salt in now-empty pot. Lock lid into place and close pressure-release valve. Select high pressure-cook function and cook for 3 minutes. Turn off Instant Pot and quick-release pressure. Carefully remove lid, allowing steam to escape away from you. Fluff bulgur gently with fork and divide among individual serving bowls. Arrange pork and pickled carrots over bulgur and top with parsley-pepita mixture. Serve.

CREAMY PARMESAN POLENTA
WITH Eggplant, Sausage, and Tomatoes

1 cup coarse-ground cornmeal

¼ teaspoon table salt

¼ teaspoon pepper, divided

2 ounces Parmesan cheese, grated (1 cup), plus extra for serving

2 tablespoons extra-virgin olive oil

1 pound hot or sweet Italian sausage, casings removed

½ eggplant (8 ounces), cut into ½-inch pieces

1 small onion, chopped fine

4 garlic cloves, minced

¼ teaspoon red pepper flakes

8 ounces cherry tomatoes, halved

¼ cup chopped fresh basil, plus extra for serving

WHY THIS RECIPE WORKS Instant Pots are wonderful for cooking polenta without the fuss of constant stirring. With a foil sling, we lowered a dish of polenta into the pot so that the steam and high pressure could render the cornmeal tender and its starches luxuriously creamy. While the polenta rested, we used the sauté function to make a topping of Italian sausage as the base, fiber-full eggplant as the body, and juicy cherry tomatoes and aromatic basil as the finish. Coarse-ground degerminated cornmeal such as yellow grits (with uniform grains the size of couscous) works best. Avoid instant or quick-cooking products, as well as whole-grain, stone-ground, or regular cornmeal. You will need a 1½-quart round soufflé dish or a ceramic dish of similar size for this recipe.

---

1 Arrange trivet included with Instant Pot in base of insert, and add 1 cup water. Fold sheet of aluminum foil into 16 by 6-inch sling, then rest 1½-quart round soufflé dish in center of sling. Whisk 4 cups water, cornmeal, salt, and ⅛ teaspoon pepper together in soufflé dish. Using sling, carefully lower soufflé dish into pot and onto trivet; allow narrow edges of sling to rest along sides of insert.

2 Lock lid into place and close pressure-release valve. Select high pressure-cook function and cook for 40 minutes. Turn off Instant Pot and quick-release pressure. Carefully remove lid, allowing steam to escape away from you.

3 Using sling, carefully transfer soufflé dish to wire rack; remove trivet and discard remaining water in pot. Whisk Parmesan into polenta, smoothing out any lumps, and let sit until thickened slightly, about 10 minutes. Season with salt and pepper to taste.

4 Meanwhile, using highest sauté function, heat oil in now-empty Instant Pot until shimmering. Add sausage and cook, breaking up meat with wooden spoon, until lightly browned, about 5 minutes. Stir in eggplant, onion, and remaining ⅛ teaspoon pepper and

Serves 4
Calories 420
Total Time 1½ hours

cook until vegetables are softened, 5 to 10 minutes. Stir in garlic and pepper flakes and cook until fragrant, about 30 seconds. Add tomatoes and cook, stirring often and scraping up any browned bits, until tomatoes are softened and begin to release their juices, about 2 minutes.

Turn off Instant Pot. Stir in basil and season with salt and pepper to taste.

5   Divide polenta among individual serving plates, top with eggplant mixture, and sprinkle with extra Parmesan and basil. Serve.

ABGOOSHT

1½ tablespoons table salt, for brining

8 ounces (1¼ cups) dried chickpeas, picked over and rinsed

2 pounds lamb shoulder chops (blade or round bone), ¾ to 1 inch thick, trimmed

1 pound Yukon Gold potatoes, peeled and quartered

2 tomatoes, cored and quartered

1 onion, quartered

1 tablespoon tomato paste

2 limu omani

2 garlic cloves, lightly crushed and peeled

2 teaspoons table salt

1 teaspoon pepper

1 teaspoon ground turmeric

½ cinnamon stick

Pinch saffron threads

3 cups fresh dill, mint, and/or tarragon leaves

4 scallions, sliced thin

8 radishes, trimmed and sliced thin

1 small red onion, halved and sliced thin

6 lavash

WHY THIS RECIPE WORKS Dating back centuries, Abgoosht is a rustic Persian stew of lamb and chickpeas that is one of the oldest and most beloved forms of wholesome one-pot comfort food. It consists of lamb cooked with nutty chickpeas, silky potatoes, a fresh tomato, and a whole onion. Enhanced with warm spices, (turmeric and a cinnamon stick) abgoosht gets its most unique flavor from limu omani (dried Persian limes). The earthy, citrusy tang of the dried rind delivers a sweetness, sourness, and muskiness that is distinctly Persian. Once cooked, the solids are mashed into a savory paste that is served alongside the broth. The lamb mash is eaten on pieces of lavash and adorned with fresh herbs, scallions, sliced radishes, pickles, and raw onion. In Iran, Abgoosht is so synonymous with being one-pot that it is sometimes called "dizi," which refers to the traditional stoneware pot in which it was prepared and served. Dizi can also mean a kind of teahouse (popular for smoking and chatting) that stews a vat of abgoosht for lunch and serves it cheaply to anyone who stops by. Abgoosht has a long reputation as a staple for poor families because back when families were large and their access to meat small, stewing lamb and mashing it with nutrient-rich foods extended the meat to every family member. Nowadays, abgoosht has increased status, as high-end restaurants have cropped up that specialize in abgoosht, offering a traditional experience, eating out of individual dizi pots and mashing your own food tableside. While abgoosht was originally made in dizi pots and took all day to cook, home cooks have been enjoying the speed of pressure cookers for decades. As the technology continues to advance, Instant Pots have become the next logical vessel with their faster cook times due to no steam escaping during cooking. The Instant Pot makes this as simple as combining everything, covering it with water, cooking it under pressure, then straining out the solids for mashing. Once we added the liquid back to the pot, the sauté function provided a gentle simmer to flavor and color the broth with a pinch of saffron. The final meal is a delicious and nutritious spread for the entire family (and then some).

Serves 6
Calories 570
Total Time 2 hours, plus
8 hours brining

To serve, place bowls of soup and platters of lamb mixture, lavash, radishes, onion, scallions, and herbs on the table and allow diners to combine components to their taste. If you cannot find limu omani in a store or online, substitute 2 tablespoons lime juice.

1   Dissolve 1½ tablespoons salt in 2 quarts cold water in large container. Add chickpeas and soak at room temperature for at least 8 hours or up to 24 hours. Drain and rinse well.

2   Add chickpeas, 7 cups water, lamb, potatoes, tomatoes, onion, tomato paste, limu omani, garlic, salt, pepper, turmeric, and cinnamon stick to Instant Pot. Lock lid into place and close pressure-release valve. Select high pressure-cook function and cook for 40 minutes. Turn off Instant Pot and let pressure release naturally for 15 minutes. Quick-release any remaining pressure, then carefully remove lid, allowing steam to escape away from you.

3   Using slotted spoon, transfer large pieces of lamb and vegetables to large bowl. Strain soup through fine-mesh strainer into separate large bowl or container; discard bones, limu omani, and cinnamon stick. Transfer strained solids to bowl with lamb and vegetables.

4   Return soup to now-empty pot. Using highest sauté function, bring soup to simmer, then turn off Instant Pot. Stir in saffron and let steep for 5 minutes. Season with salt and pepper to taste.

5   Using potato masher, mash lamb mixture until meat is finely shredded and chickpeas and vegetables are mostly smooth. Season with salt and pepper to taste, and transfer to serving platter. Ladle soup into individual serving bowls and serve with lamb mixture, fresh herbs, scallions, radishes, red onion, and lavash.

photo on following page >

Abgoosht, page 90

LAMB MEATBALLS
WITH Creamy Lemon and Feta Orzo

¼ cup milk

3 tablespoons panko bread crumbs

1 small fennel bulb, 2 tablespoons fronds minced, divided, stalks discarded, bulb halved, cored, and chopped fine

2 teaspoons grated lemon zest, divided

½ teaspoon table salt, divided

1 pound ground lamb

2 teaspoons extra-virgin olive oil

12 ounces Swiss chard, stems chopped fine, leaves chopped into 1-inch pieces

2 cups 100 percent whole-wheat orzo

3 garlic cloves, minced

2 cups chicken broth

1¼ cups water

1 ounce feta cheese, crumbled (¼ cup)

WHY THIS RECIPE WORKS This dish, ready in just 45 minutes, combines tender lamb meatballs with creamy orzo pasta, along with an abundance of fresh fennel and Swiss chard. For tender, aromatic meatballs, in addition to a simple panade (a mixture of milk and bread crumbs that helps keep meatballs moist), we added fragrant lemon zest and minced fennel fronds to the ground lamb. Shaping the mixture into 1½-inch meatballs gave us the perfect size to finish cooking in the 2 minutes it took to cook the orzo. For the base of the dish, we sautéed chopped fennel and Swiss chard stems before adding garlic and the orzo. We sautéed the orzo until lightly toasted, which helped it maintain a pleasant chew and keep the grains distinct while cooking under pressure. After releasing the pressure, we stirred chopped Swiss chard leaves and a touch more lemon zest gently into the orzo and then let everything sit until the chard was wilted and the orzo was creamy. A sprinkle of minced fennel fronds and tangy crumbled feta cheese was a tasty and welcome finish. Traditional orzo can be substituted for the whole-wheat orzo, if desired. If your fennel bulb does not come with fronds, substitute 2 tablespoons chopped fresh dill or parsley for the fronds.

---

1 Using fork, mash milk and panko to paste in large bowl. Stir in 1 tablespoon fennel fronds, 1 teaspoon lemon zest, and ¼ teaspoon salt. Add lamb and knead with hands until thoroughly combined. Pinch off and roll mixture into twelve 1½-inch meatballs.

2 Using highest sauté function, heat oil in Instant Pot until shimmering. Add chopped fennel and chard stems and cook until softened, 3 to 5 minutes.

3 Stir in orzo and garlic and cook until fragrant, about 30 seconds. Stir in broth, water, and remaining ¼ teaspoon salt, scraping up any browned bits, then arrange meatballs

Serves 4
Calories 670
Total Time 45 minutes

in even layer in pot. Lock lid into place and close pressure-release valve. Select high pressure-cook function and cook for 2 minutes. Turn off Instant Pot and quick-release pressure. Carefully remove lid, allowing steam to escape away from you.

4 Gently stir in chard leaves and remaining 1 teaspoon lemon zest. Partially cover pot and let sit until chard is wilted and sauce thickens slightly, about 5 minutes. Season with salt and pepper to taste. Sprinkle individual portions with feta and remaining 1 tablespoon fennel fronds before serving.

CHAPTER 3

SEAFOOD

98   New England Fish Chowder

101   Swordfish Stew with Tomatoes, Capers, and Pine Nuts

102   Calamari, Chorizo, and Chickpea Stew

104   Salmon Niçoise Salad

108   Salmon with Spiced Chickpea, Cucumber, and Tomato Salad

110   Salmon with Wild Rice and Orange Salad

113   Salmon with Ponzu-Braised Eggplant

114   Haddock with Tomatoes, Escarole, and Crispy Garlic

116   Swordfish with Braised Green Beans, Tomatoes, and Feta

118   Halibut with Lentils, Kale, and Pancetta

120   Halibut with Couscous and Ras el Hanout

122   Southwestern Shrimp and Oat Berry Bowl

125   Shrimp and White Beans with Butternut Squash and Sage

126   Shrimp Jambalaya

128   Mussels with Red Curry and Coconut Rice

NEW ENGLAND FISH CHOWDER

6 slices bacon, cut into ½-inch pieces

1 pound leeks, halved lengthwise, sliced ½ inch thick, and washed thoroughly

1 tablespoon extra-virgin olive oil

1½ teaspoons minced fresh thyme or ½ teaspoon dried

3 cups water

1½ pounds Yukon Gold potatoes, peeled and cut into ½-inch pieces

1 bay leaf

1 teaspoon table salt

2 cups whole milk

1 tablespoon cornstarch

½ teaspoon pepper

2 cups fresh or frozen corn

1½ pounds skinless cod fillets, 1 to 1½ inches thick, cut into 2-inch pieces

2 tablespoons minced fresh chives

WHY THIS RECIPE WORKS While some chowders are heavy and cream-laden, we opted for a much lighter soup that allowed the flavor of gently poached cod to shine through in a clean, thyme-scented broth. Just a little bit of bacon fat (rendered using the sauté function) infused the whole dish with richness and created a smoky base for our aromatics. For a high-impact garnish, we reserved the crisped bacon to sprinkle over individual servings. We largely relied on potatoes (rather than heavy cream or crackers) to thicken and add texture to the chowder, as the Instant Pot's pressure function quickly turned raw potatoes and water into a starch-laden broth in which we could delicately cook the fish. Poaching the cod off-heat minimized the risk of overcooking and resulted in perfect fish that paired beautifully with smoky bacon, sweet corn, and oniony chives. Black sea bass, haddock, hake, and pollock are good substitutes for the cod.

1 Using highest sauté function, cook bacon in Instant Pot until browned and fat is well rendered, 6 to 8 minutes. Using slotted spoon, transfer bacon to paper towel–lined plate; set aside for serving.

2 Add leeks, oil, and thyme to fat left in pot and cook, stirring occasionally, until leeks are softened and lightly browned, 3 to 5 minutes. Stir in water, scraping up any browned bits, then stir in potatoes, bay leaf, and salt. Lock lid into place and close pressure-release valve. Select high pressure-cook function and cook for 3 minutes.

3 Turn off Instant Pot and quick-release pressure. Carefully remove lid, allowing steam to escape away from you. Whisk milk, cornstarch, and pepper together in bowl. Whisk milk mixture and corn into potato mixture in pot and cook, using highest sauté function, until liquid is slightly thickened, about 1 minute. Turn off Instant Pot.

4 Submerge cod in cooking liquid, partially cover pot, and let sit until cod flakes apart when gently prodded with paring knife, 5 to 8 minutes; discard bay leaf. Break up any remaining large pieces of cod. Season with salt and pepper to taste. Sprinkle individual portions with bacon and chives before serving.

Serves 4 to 6
Calories 320
Total Time 45 minutes

SWORDFISH STEW
WITH Tomatoes, Capers, and Pine Nuts

WHY THIS RECIPE WORKS This Sicilian-inspired stew is the ultimate balance of sweet, sour, and salty notes. We chose swordfish for its meaty texture that could stand up to a symphony of bold flavors that do well in the Instant Pot, as their tastes and textures resist blowing out under pressure. For the base, we created a stock of onions, garlic, thyme, and red pepper flakes simmered in white wine, tomatoes, and clam juice. We mixed in golden raisins and capers to provide contrasting sweet notes and briny bursts of flavor. After just 1 minute under pressure, the swordfish emerged tender and succulent. To top our stew, we combined orange zest, mint, and garlic, with pine nuts for crunch. Halibut, mahi-mahi, red snapper, and striped bass are good substitutes for the swordfish. If the swordfish has not reached at least 130 degrees after releasing the pressure, partially cover the pot and continue to cook using residual heat until it reaches 130 degrees. Serve with crusty bread.

2 tablespoons extra-virgin olive oil

2 onions, chopped fine

1 teaspoon minced fresh thyme or ¼ teaspoon dried

Pinch red pepper flakes

4 garlic cloves, minced, divided

1 (8-ounce) bottle clam juice

¼ cup dry white wine

1 (28-ounce) can whole peeled tomatoes, drained with juice reserved, chopped coarse

¼ cup golden raisins

2 tablespoons capers, rinsed

½ teaspoon table salt

½ teaspoon pepper

1½ pounds skinless swordfish steaks, 1 to 1½ inches thick, cut into 1-inch pieces

¼ cup pine nuts, toasted

¼ cup minced fresh mint

1 teaspoon grated orange zest

1   Using highest sauté function, heat oil in Instant Pot until shimmering. Add onions and cook until softened and lightly browned, 3 to 5 minutes. Add thyme, pepper flakes, and three-quarters of garlic and cook, stirring frequently, until fragrant, about 30 seconds.

2   Stir in clam juice and wine, scraping up any browned bits, then stir in tomatoes and reserved juice, raisins, capers, salt, and pepper. Arrange swordfish pieces in even layer in pot and spoon some cooking liquid over top.

3   Lock lid into place and close pressure-release valve. Select high pressure-cook function and cook for 1 minute. Turn off Instant Pot and quick-release pressure. Carefully remove lid, allowing steam to escape away from you.

4   Combine pine nuts, mint, orange zest, and remaining garlic in bowl. Season stew with salt and pepper to taste. Sprinkle individual portions with pine nut mixture before serving.

CALAMARI, CHORIZO, AND CHICKPEA STEW

1½ tablespoons table salt for brining

8 ounces (1¼ cups) dried chickpeas, picked over and rinsed

1 tablespoon extra-virgin olive oil, plus extra for drizzling

2 red bell peppers, stemmed, seeded, and chopped

1 onion, chopped

6 ounces Spanish semicured chorizo sausage, sliced ¼ inch thick

4 garlic cloves, minced

2 teaspoons hot smoked paprika

½ cup dry red wine

1 (28-ounce) can diced tomatoes

1 pound squid, bodies sliced crosswise into ¾-inch-thick rings, tentacles halved

1 cup chicken broth

5 ounces (5 cups) baby spinach

1½ teaspoons red wine vinegar

WHY THIS RECIPE WORKS Squid is a perfect healthy protein because it is versatile and packed with omega-3s. According to a cooking school adage, squid should be cooked for 1 minute or 1 hour; anything in between results in tough squid. In other words, it is best medium-rare or truly braised. In just 20 minutes, the Instant Pot pressure-braised the squid, which was a wonderful addition to the Catalan combo of chickpeas and spinach. We started by softening red peppers and onions, adding chorizo to render flavorful fat. Stirring in some hot smoked paprika before deglazing with red wine and adding diced tomatoes produced a smoky, spicy broth. If hot smoked paprika is unavailable, substitute 1¾ teaspoons sweet smoked paprika and ¼ teaspoon cayenne pepper.

---

1 Dissolve 1½ tablespoons salt in 2 quarts cold water in large container. Add chickpeas and soak at room temperature for at least 8 hours or up to 24 hours. Drain and rinse well.

2 Using highest sauté function, heat oil in Instant Pot until shimmering. Add bell peppers, onion, and chorizo and cook until vegetables are softened and lightly browned, and chorizo is lightly browned, 7 to 9 minutes. Add garlic and paprika and cook, stirring frequently, until fragrant, about 30 seconds.

3 Stir in wine, scraping up any browned bits, and cook until mostly evaporated, about 1 minute. Stir in chickpeas, tomatoes and their juice, squid, and broth. Lock lid into place and close pressure-release valve. Select high pressure-cook function and cook for 20 minutes.

4 Turn off Instant Pot and quick-release pressure. Carefully remove lid, allowing steam to escape away from you. Stir in spinach and let sit until wilted, about 1 minute. Stir in vinegar and season with salt and pepper to taste. Drizzle individual portions with extra oil before serving.

Serves 4 to 6
Calories 390
Total Time 1 hour, plus 8 hours brining

SALMON NIÇOISE SALAD

8 ounces haricots verts or green beans, trimmed

¾ teaspoon table salt, divided, plus salt for cooking vegetables

1 pound small red potatoes, unpeeled, halved

4 large eggs

1 (1-pound) skinless salmon fillet, 1 to 1½ inches thick

3 tablespoons extra-virgin olive oil

2 tablespoons lemon juice

2 tablespoons chopped fresh basil

1 teaspoon Dijon mustard

1 small shallot, minced

1 head Bibb lettuce (8 ounces), leaves separated

8 ounces cherry tomatoes, halved

½ cup pitted kalamata olives, halved

WHY THIS RECIPE WORKS This quintessentially hearty salad is the Instant Pot's magic trick, cooking no less than four discrete elements all within the pot. Traditional French salade niçoise is incredibly vibrant and protein-packed with its mix of vegetables, hard-cooked eggs, olives, and canned tuna. For our version, we swapped out tuna for skinless salmon, which kept the classic flavors of this dish intact while giving us a fresher, meatier protein. Whether a true niçoise can include cooked vegetables has been debated, but we prefer the version popularized by Julia Child, which has boiled potatoes and warm green beans. Delicious but unquestionably fussy, salade niçoise requires all items to be prepared separately and cooked individually. If one cooking vessel is used, green beans are boiled first, followed by potatoes and then eggs, with each item needing to be either entirely drained or removed between each step. If separate pots are used, careful monitoring is necessary to monitor cooking times and avoid overcooking any of the items. And then there's the additional step of searing the salmon before assembling everything long after cooking the first item. The Instant Pot does away with this juggling, cooking practically everything at once. We used the high sauté function to cook our haricots verts to a perfect crisp-tender. After removing them from the pot, we used the remaining water to cook our potatoes, eggs, and salmon simultaneously. We layered the potatoes and eggs on the bottom, enabling us to rest the salmon gently in a sling on top. In only 5 minutes under pressure, these elements were warm and tender. A tangy dressing brought this new niçoise together; we tossed a small amount with the lettuce for even distribution, saving the rest for drizzling after assembling the salad. We topped the greens with cherry tomatoes and olives, along with our flaked salmon, haricots verts, and quartered eggs, to round out this bright, rich, warm, fresh, and crunchy meal. We dare you to find a more creative use for your Instant Pot.

Use small red potatoes measuring 1 to 2 inches in diameter. This recipe works best with farmed salmon; we do not recommend using wild salmon. If the salmon has not reached at least 125 degrees (for medium-rare) after releasing the pressure, partially cover the pot and continue to cook using residual heat until it reaches 125 degrees.

1 Using highest sauté function, bring 1 quart water to boil in Instant Pot. Fill large bowl halfway with ice and water. Add haricots verts and 2 teaspoons salt to boiling water and cook until haricots verts are crisp-tender, 5 to 7 minutes. Turn off Instant Pot. Using slotted spoon, transfer haricots verts to prepared ice bath, let sit for 5 minutes, then transfer to paper towel–lined plate; do not discard ice bath.

2 Arrange potatoes in even layer in water remaining in pot, then arrange eggs on top of potatoes. Fold sheet of aluminum foil into 16 by 6-inch sling. Place salmon skinned side down in center of sling and sprinkle with ½ teaspoon salt. Using sling, lower salmon into pot on top of eggs; allow narrow edges of sling to rest along sides of pot.

3 Lock lid into place and close pressure-release valve. Select high pressure-cook function and cook for 5 minutes. Turn off Instant Pot and quick-release pressure. Carefully remove lid, allowing steam to escape away from you. Using sling, transfer salmon to large plate and let cool slightly.

4 Add ice to prepared ice bath as needed. Using tongs, transfer eggs to ice bath and let sit for 5 minutes. Drain potatoes in colander and let cool slightly. Peel eggs and quarter lengthwise. Flake salmon into large 2-inch pieces.

5 Whisk oil, lemon juice, basil, mustard, shallot, and remaining ¼ teaspoon salt together in small bowl, then transfer 2 tablespoons dressing to large bowl. Add lettuce, toss to coat with dressing, and season with salt and pepper to taste. Transfer lettuce to serving platter and top with tomatoes, olives, haricots verts, potatoes, eggs, and salmon. Drizzle with reserved dressing. Serve.

photo on following page >

Salmon Niçoise Salad,
page 104

SALMON WITH SPICED CHICKPEA, CUCUMBER, AND Tomato Salad

⅓ cup extra-virgin olive oil, divided

1 tablespoon garam masala

½ cup water

2 (15-ounce) cans chickpeas, rinsed

½ teaspoon table salt, plus salt for cooking chickpeas

4 (6-ounce) skinless salmon fillets, 1 to 1½ inches thick

¼ teaspoon pepper

1 shallot, minced

1 teaspoon grated lemon zest plus 2 tablespoons juice

1 English cucumber, halved lengthwise and sliced thin

8 ounces cherry tomatoes, halved

¼ cup coarsely chopped fresh mint

WHY THIS RECIPE WORKS Succulent salmon paired with a simple salad lends itself well to Instant Pot cooking. We bloomed garam masala in oil and added canned chickpeas. While the salmon cooked in a sling above, the chickpeas warmed through and absorbed the spices. After draining the pot, we combined the chickpeas with crunchy cucumbers and tomatoes and a quick dressing of oil, shallot, and lemon juice, which offered complex flavors and textures. This recipe works best with farmed salmon; we do not recommend using wild salmon. If the salmon has not reached at least 125 degrees (for medium-rare) after releasing the pressure, partially cover the pot and continue to cook using residual heat until it reaches 125 degrees.

1 Using highest sauté function, heat 1 tablespoon oil and garam masala in Instant Pot until fragrant, about 1 minute. Turn off Instant Pot. Stir in water, scraping up any browned bits, then stir in chickpeas and ¼ teaspoon salt.

2 Fold sheet of aluminum foil into 16 by 6-inch sling. Arrange salmon skinned side down in center of sling and sprinkle with salt and pepper. Using sling, lower salmon into pot on top of chickpea mixture; allow narrow edges of sling to rest along sides of pot.

3 Lock lid into place and close pressure-release valve. Select high pressure-cook function and cook for 3 minutes. Meanwhile, whisk shallot, lemon zest and juice, and remaining oil together in large bowl. Add cucumber, tomatoes, and mint and toss to combine.

4 Turn off Instant Pot and quick-release pressure. Carefully remove lid, allowing steam to escape away from you. Using sling, transfer salmon to large plate. Strain chickpeas; discard cooking liquid. Transfer chickpeas to bowl with cucumber mixture, toss to combine, and season with salt and pepper to taste. Serve salmon with salad.

Serves 4
Calories 540
Total Time 30 minutes

SALMON WITH WILD RICE
AND Orange Salad

1 cup wild rice, picked over and rinsed

3 tablespoons extra-virgin olive oil, divided

½ teaspoon table salt, plus salt for cooking rice

2 oranges, divided, plus ⅛ teaspoon grated orange zest

1 small shallot, minced

1 tablespoon red wine vinegar

2 teaspoons Dijon mustard

1 teaspoon honey

2 carrots, peeled and shredded

¼ cup chopped fresh mint

4 (6-ounce) skinless salmon fillets, 1 to 1½ inches thick

1 teaspoon ground dried Aleppo pepper

WHY THIS RECIPE WORKS Wild rice is a cultivated aquatic grass that we love for its high nutritional value and woodsy earthiness. It typically can take an hour to cook, but the Instant Pot slashed that time in half, during which we prepared additional ingredients for a vibrant wild rice salad studded with juicy oranges and sweet shredded carrots. A generous sprinkling of ground Aleppo pepper gave our salmon a uniquely fruity touch of heat that complemented the nutty, citrusy flavors in the salad. Do not use quick-cooking or presteamed wild rice in this recipe. If Aleppo pepper is unavailable, you can substitute ¾ teaspoon paprika plus ¼ teaspoon red pepper flakes. This recipe works best with farmed salmon; we do not recommend using wild salmon. If the salmon has not reached at least 125 degrees (for medium-rare) after releasing the pressure, partially cover the pot and continue to cook using residual heat until it reaches 125 degrees.

---

1 Combine 6 cups water, rice, 1 tablespoon oil, and 1½ teaspoons salt in Instant Pot. Lock lid into place and close pressure-release valve. Select high pressure-cook function and cook for 15 minutes.

2 Turn off Instant Pot and let pressure release naturally for 15 minutes. Quick-release any remaining pressure, then carefully remove lid, allowing steam to escape away from you. Drain rice and set aside to cool slightly. Wipe pot clean with paper towels.

3 Cut away peel and pith from 1 orange. Quarter orange, then slice crosswise into ¼-inch pieces. Whisk orange zest, shallot, vinegar, mustard, honey, and remaining 2 tablespoons oil together in large bowl. Add rice, orange pieces, carrots, and mint; toss to combine; and season with salt and pepper to taste; set aside for serving.

4 Fold sheet of aluminum foil into 16 by 6-inch sling. Slice remaining 1 orange ¼ inch thick and shingle widthwise in 3 rows across center of sling. Arrange salmon skinned side down on top

Serves 4
Calories 680
Total Time 1 hour

of orange slices and sprinkle with Aleppo pepper and salt. Add ½ cup water to now-empty pot. Using sling, lower salmon into pot; allow narrow edges of sling to rest along sides of pot. Lock lid into place and close pressure-release valve. Select high pressure-cook function and cook for 3 minutes.

5   Turn off Instant Pot and quick-release pressure. Carefully remove lid, allowing steam to escape away from you. Using sling, transfer salmon to large plate. Gently lift and tilt fillets with spatula to remove orange slices. Serve salmon with salad.

Serves 4
Calories 490
Total Time 45 minutes

SALMON WITH PONZU-BRAISED EGGPLANT

WHY THIS RECIPE WORKS Braised eggplant is a popular dish in Japan, where it is prepared with soy sauce, bonito flakes, and citrus. Bottled ponzu has all these umami flavors, making it a great base for a flavor-packed sauce. We love the versatility of eggplant and salmon, so we teamed them up for a complete meal. In 1 minute, the Instant Pot's produced juicy fish and creamy eggplant (a foil sling kept the salmon intact while it cooked). We let the eggplant continue to cook in the residual heat for another 2 minutes so that it could thicken into a luscious coating. This recipe works best with farmed salmon; we do not recommend using wild salmon. If the salmon has not reached at least 125 degrees (for medium-rare) after sitting in step 3, return cover and continue to cook using residual heat until it reaches 125 degrees.

½ cup water

¼ cup ponzu

1 tablespoon honey

1 tablespoon mirin

1 teaspoon cornstarch

1 tablespoon canola oil

3 scallions, white and green parts separated and sliced thin

3 garlic cloves, minced

1 tablespoon grated fresh ginger

2 pounds eggplant, cut into 2-inch pieces

1½ pounds skinless salmon fillets, 1 to 1½ inches thick, cut into 2-inch pieces

¼ teaspoon salt

¼ teaspoon pepper

1 tablespoon sesame seeds, toasted

1   Whisk water, ponzu sauce, honey, mirin, and cornstarch together in bowl; set aside. Combine oil, scallion whites, garlic, and ginger in Instant Pot and cook, using highest sauté function, until fragrant, about 3 minutes. Turn off Instant Pot. Stir in ponzu mixture, scraping up any browned bits, then arrange eggplant in even layer in pot.

2   Fold sheet of aluminum foil into 16 by 6-inch sling. Arrange salmon skinned side down in center of sling and sprinkle with salt and pepper. Using sling, lower salmon into pot on top of eggplant; allow narrow edges of sling to rest along sides of pot. Lock lid into place and close pressure-release valve. Select high pressure-cook function and cook for 1 minute.

3   Turn off Instant Pot and quick-release pressure. Carefully remove lid, allowing steam to escape away from you. Partially cover pot with lid and let salmon and eggplant sit for 2 minutes. Using sling, transfer salmon to large plate. Stir eggplant to coat with sauce. Serve salmon with eggplant, sprinkling individual portions with scallion greens and sesame seeds.

HADDOCK WITH TOMATOES, ESCAROLE, AND Crispy Garlic

3 tablespoons extra-virgin olive oil, divided, plus extra for drizzling

4 garlic cloves, sliced thin

1 head escarole (1 pound), trimmed and cut into 1-inch pieces

¾ teaspoon table salt, divided

12 ounces cherry tomatoes, halved

1 cup dry white wine

2 sprigs fresh thyme

¼ teaspoon red pepper flakes

4 (6-ounce) skinless haddock fillets, 1 to 1½ inches thick

¼ teaspoon pepper

3 tablespoons chopped fresh parsley

WHY THIS RECIPE WORKS Stovetop methods for steaming fish require monitoring to prevent overcooking. The Instant Pot—with its consistent moisture level and temperature (and precise timing)—guarantees foolproof results that are easy to get every time. We chose flaky haddock and paired it with white wine, cherry tomatoes, thyme, and red pepper flakes. The wine and tomatoes provided enough liquid to steam the fish and create a clean, aromatic serving broth at the same time. A foil sling allowed the fish to flavor the broth while enabling us to easily transfer the cooked fish to a serving platter without falling apart. To bulk up our dish, we turned to fiber-rich escarole, which cooked quickly and was a pleasantly bitter pairing with the fish. To amp up flavor, we cooked the escarole in an infused oil that we made by crisping thinly sliced garlic in the pot. Served with crusty bread to soak up the broth, dinner was ready. Black sea bass, cod, hake, and pollock are good substitutes for the haddock. Tail-end fillets can be folded for proper thickness. If the haddock has not reached at least 135 degrees after releasing the pressure, partially cover the pot and continue to cook using residual heat until it reaches 135 degrees.

1 Using highest sauté function, heat 2 tablespoons oil in Instant Pot until shimmering. Add garlic and cook, stirring often, until beginning to brown, 2 to 3 minutes. Turn off Instant Pot and continue to cook, using residual heat, until garlic is evenly golden brown and crisp, 2 to 3 minutes. Using slotted spoon, transfer garlic to paper towel–lined plate; set aside for serving.

2 Add escarole and ¼ teaspoon salt to oil left in pot and cook, using highest sauté function, until wilted, 2 to 4 minutes. Turn off Instant Pot. Transfer escarole to bowl and cover to keep warm.

3 Add tomatoes, wine, thyme sprigs, and pepper flakes to now-empty pot. Fold sheet of aluminum foil into 16 by 6-inch sling. Arrange haddock skinned side down in center of sling,

Serves 4
Calories 310
Total Time 45 minutes

brush with remaining 1 tablespoon oil, and sprinkle with pepper and remaining ½ teaspoon salt. Using sling, lower haddock into pot on top of tomato mixture; allow narrow edges of sling to rest along sides of pot.

4   Lock lid into place and close pressure-release valve. Select high pressure-cook function and cook for 4 minutes. Turn off Instant Pot and

quick-release pressure. Carefully remove lid, allowing steam to escape away from you. Using sling, transfer haddock to large plate.

5   Discard thyme sprigs from tomato mixture. Stir in parsley and season with salt to taste. Serve haddock with escarole and tomato mixture, sprinkling individual portions with garlic and drizzling with extra oil.

SWORDFISH WITH BRAISED GREEN BEANS, TOMATOES AND Feta

1 tablespoon extra-virgin olive oil, plus extra for drizzling

1 onion, chopped fine

3 garlic cloves, minced

1½ teaspoons chopped fresh oregano or ½ teaspoon dried

¼ teaspoon red pepper flakes

1 (28-ounce) can whole peeled tomatoes, drained with juice reserved, halved

1 pound Yukon Gold potatoes, cut into ½-inch pieces

12 ounces green beans, trimmed

¼ teaspoon table salt, divided

4 (6-ounce) skinless swordfish steaks, 1 to 1½ inches thick

2 tablespoons chopped pitted kalamata olives

2 tablespoons chopped fresh mint, plus extra for serving

1 ounce feta cheese, crumbled (¼ cup)

WHY THIS RECIPE WORKS This recipe combines a few simple ingredients and transforms them into a rich and satisfying dish full of flavor while remaining low in calories. We love swordfish because it packs big, meaty flavor and is high in minerals. Thanks to the Instant Pot's intense heat, canned whole peeled tomatoes and their juice transformed into a concentrated broth. As raw potatoes simmered in the liquid, they gave off starches to help thicken it, while green beans melted into tender bites. To keep the swordfish from overcooking, we placed it above the liquid and basted it with sauce just before going under pressure. A smattering of olives and feta, added at the end of cooking so their flavor wouldn't dominate the dish, offered pleasant briny bites. A garnish of fresh mint added a clean finish. Halibut, mahi-mahi, red snapper, and striped bass are good substitutes for the swordfish. If the swordfish has not reached at least 130 degrees after releasing the pressure, partially cover the pot and continue to cook using residual heat until it reaches 130 degrees.

1 Using highest sauté function, heat oil in Instant Pot until shimmering. Add onion and cook until softened and lightly browned, 3 to 5 minutes. Add garlic, oregano, and pepper flakes and cook, stirring frequently, until fragrant, about 30 seconds. Stir in tomatoes and their juice, scraping up any browned bits. Reserve ½ cup tomato mixture, then stir potatoes, green beans, and ⅛ teaspoon salt into pot.

2 Sprinkle swordfish with remaining ⅛ teaspoon salt. Nestle swordfish into pot and spoon reserved tomato mixture over tops of steaks. Lock lid into place and close pressure-release valve. Select high pressure-cook function and cook for 1 minute. Turn off Instant Pot and quick-release pressure. Carefully remove lid, allowing steam to escape away from you.

3 Using spatula, transfer swordfish to large plate. Tent with aluminum foil and let rest while finishing vegetable mixture. Using highest sauté function, cook vegetable mixture until liquid has thickened slightly, 3 to 5 minutes. Stir in olives and mint and season with salt and pepper to taste. Serve swordfish with vegetable mixture, sprinkling individual portions with feta and extra mint and drizzling with extra oil.

HALIBUT WITH LENTILS, KALE,
AND Pancetta

2 tablespoons extra-virgin olive oil, divided, plus extra for drizzling

1 onion, chopped fine

2 carrots, peeled and chopped fine

2 ounces pancetta, chopped fine

2 garlic cloves, minced

½ teaspoon minced fresh thyme or ⅛ teaspoon dried

2 cups water

1 cup lentilles du Puy, picked over and rinsed

½ teaspoon table salt, divided

12 ounces kale, stemmed and chopped

4 (6-ounce) skinless halibut fillets, 1 to 1½ inches thick

¼ teaspoon pepper

½ cup panko bread crumbs

2 tablespoons chopped fresh parsley

½ teaspoon grated lemon zest, plus 1 tablespoon juice

WHY THIS RECIPE WORKS A steaming plate of lentils, smoky pancetta, and a perfectly cooked halibut fillet with crispy bread crumbs—that's one hearty meal. We started by sautéing pancetta, onion, carrots, garlic, and thyme for the base. The even cooking of the Instant Pot allowed the lentils to keep their tender-firm texture for a healthful, stew-y dish. Placing kale on top of the lentils to cook let it wilt but not overcook. For all components to finish cooking simultaneously, we suspended the halibut in a foil sling above the lentils and kale before they were done, and then cooked everything together for 2 more minutes. A sprinkle of lemony bread crumbs on top finished the dish. Lentilles du Puy, also called French green lentils, are our first choice, but brown, black, or regular green lentils will work (cook times will vary). Mahi-mahi, red snapper, striped bass, and swordfish are good substitutes for the halibut. If the fish has not reached at least 130 degrees after releasing the pressure, partially cover the pot and continue to cook using residual heat until it reaches 130 degrees. Serve with lemon wedges.

---

1 Using highest sauté function, heat 1 tablespoon oil in Instant Pot until shimmering. Add onion, carrots, and pancetta and cook until vegetables are softened and lightly browned, and pancetta is lightly browned, 4 to 6 minutes. Add garlic and thyme and cook, stirring frequently, until fragrant, about 30 seconds. Stir in water, scraping up any browned bits, then stir in lentils and ¼ teaspoon salt. Arrange kale in even layer on top of lentils.

2 Lock lid into place and close pressure-release valve. Select high pressure-cook function and cook for 12 minutes. Turn off Instant Pot and quick-release pressure. Carefully remove lid, allowing steam to escape away from you.

3 Stir lentils and kale gently to combine. Fold sheet of aluminum foil into 16 by 6-inch sling. Arrange halibut skinned side down in center of sling and sprinkle with pepper and remaining

Serves 4
Calories 480
Total Time 1 hour

¼ teaspoon salt. Using sling, lower halibut into pot on top of lentil mixture; allow narrow edges of sling to rest along sides of pot.

4 Lock lid into place and close pressure-release valve. Select high pressure-cook function and cook for 2 minutes. Turn off Instant Pot and quick-release pressure. Carefully remove lid, allowing steam to escape away from you. Using sling, transfer halibut to large plate.

5 Meanwhile, toss panko with remaining 1 tablespoon oil in bowl until evenly coated. Microwave, stirring frequently, until light golden brown, 2 to 4 minutes. Let cool slightly, then stir in parsley and lemon zest; set aside for serving.

6 Stir lemon juice into lentil mixture and season with salt and pepper to taste. Serve halibut with lentils, sprinkling individual portions with bread crumb topping and drizzling with extra oil.

HALIBUT WITH COUSCOUS
<u>AND</u> Ras el Hanout

½ cup plain yogurt

2 tablespoons tahini

4 garlic cloves, minced, divided

2 lemons, plus 2 teaspoons grated lemon zest, divided, plus 1 tablespoon lemon juice

3 tablespoons extra-virgin olive oil

2 teaspoons ras el hanout

1 cup 100 percent whole-wheat couscous

1 cup jarred roasted red peppers, rinsed, patted dry, and sliced ¼ inch thick

¾ teaspoon table salt, divided

3 tablespoons chopped fresh mint, divided

4 (6-ounce) skinless halibut fillets, 1 to 1½ inches thick

¼ teaspoon pepper

¼ cup sliced almonds, toasted

WHY THIS RECIPE WORKS We love the delicate flavor of halibut, but because it is naturally low in fat, it can dry out quickly during cooking. Thanks to the Instant Pot, dry fish can be avoided. We rested the halibut on a bed of lemon slices in a foil sling, allowing us move the halibut with ease while the lemon insulated the fish from direct heat and permeated it with citrusy flavor. The consistent internal environment of the pot produced moist fish in just 2 minutes. For a Moroccan-inspired side, we turned to couscous and ras el hanout. The warm spice blend, combined with garlic and lemon, infused the couscous with complex flavor. A cool, creamy yogurt-tahini sauce was a nice contrast to the assertive couscous, while a topping of toasted almonds complemented the nuttiness of the whole-wheat couscous. If using white couscous, decrease the boiling water to 1 cup. Mahi-mahi, red snapper, striped bass, and swordfish are good substitutes for the halibut. If the fish has not reached at least 130 degrees after releasing the pressure, partially cover the pot and continue to cook using residual heat until it reaches 130 degrees.

1   Whisk yogurt, tahini, one-quarter of garlic, and 1 teaspoon lemon zest together in small bowl and season with salt and pepper to taste; set aside for serving. Microwave oil, ras el hanout, remaining garlic, and remaining 1 teaspoon lemon zest in large bowl until fragrant, about 30 seconds, stirring halfway through microwaving.

2   Stir 1½ cups boiling water, couscous, red peppers, and ½ teaspoon salt into spice mixture; cover and let sit for 10 minutes. Drizzle lemon juice over couscous and sprinkle with 2 tablespoons mint. Fluff couscous with fork and season with salt and pepper to taste; set aside for serving.

3   Meanwhile, add ½ cup water to Instant Pot. Fold sheet of aluminum foil into 16 by 6-inch sling. Slice lemons ¼ inch thick and shingle widthwise in 3 rows across center of sling. Arrange

Serves 4
Calories 540
Total Time 45 minutes

halibut skinned side down on top of lemon slices and sprinkle with pepper and remaining ¼ teaspoon salt.

4 Using sling, lower halibut into pot on top of water; allow narrow edges of sling to rest along sides of pot. Lock lid into place and close pressure-release valve. Select high pressure-cook function and cook for 2 minutes.

5 Turn off Instant Pot and quick-release pressure. Carefully remove lid, allowing steam to escape away from you. Using sling, transfer halibut to large plate. Gently lift and tilt fillets with spatula to remove lemon slices. Serve halibut with couscous, drizzling individual portions with yogurt-tahini sauce and sprinkling with almonds and remaining 1 tablespoon mint.

SOUTHWESTERN SHRIMP
AND Oat Berry Bowl

1½ cups oat berries, rinsed

3 tablespoons extra-virgin olive oil, divided

½ teaspoon table salt, divided, plus salt for cooking oat berries

1 cup frozen corn, thawed

¼ cup finely chopped red onion

1 tablespoon grated lime zest plus 1 tablespoon juice

½ cup fresh cilantro leaves

2 poblano chiles, stemmed, seeded, and sliced thin

4 garlic cloves, minced

¾ teaspoon chili powder

¾ teaspoon ground coriander

1 pound large shrimp (26 to 30 per pound), peeled, deveined, and tails removed

1 avocado, halved, pitted, and cut into ½-inch pieces

1½ ounces corn tortilla chips, broken into 1-inch pieces (½ cup)

½ recipe Chipotle-Yogurt Sauce (page 17)

WHY THIS RECIPE WORKS Oat berries (also known as groats) are a favorite healthy base for their high nutritional content, hearty chew, and pleasant nuttiness. On the stove, they can take at least 45 minutes to cook, but the high-pressure Instant Pot function cuts that in half. Inspired by the Southwestern flavors of fast-casual burrito bowls, we set out to create an elevated at-home version. We seasoned the oat berries by charring poblano peppers with garlic and spices, then tossed the two together. We seared shrimp in the same aromatics to double down on flavor. Finally, we added an abundance of toppings: corn salsa, for zesty sweetness; avocado, for rich creaminess; spicy yogurt, which gave cool heat; and salty tortilla chips to add fun crunch. Extra-large shrimp (21 to 25 per pound) also work in this recipe.

---

1 Combine 6 cups water, oat berries, 1 tablespoon oil, and 1½ teaspoons salt in Instant Pot. Lock lid into place and close pressure-release valve. Select high pressure-cook function and cook for 20 minutes.

2 Turn off Instant Pot and let pressure release naturally for 15 minutes. Quick-release any remaining pressure, then carefully remove lid, allowing steam to escape away from you. Drain oat berries, transfer to large bowl, and cover to keep warm. Wipe pot clean with paper towels.

3 Meanwhile, stir corn, onion, lime juice, cilantro, and ¼ teaspoon salt together in small bowl; set aside for serving.

4 Using highest sauté function, heat 1 tablespoon oil in now-empty pot until shimmering. Add poblanos and cook until softened and lightly browned, 3 to 5 minutes. Add lime zest, garlic, chili powder, coriander, and remaining ¼ teaspoon salt and cook, stirring frequently, until fragrant, about 30 seconds.

Serves 4
Calories 610
Total Time 1 hour

Transfer poblano mixture to bowl with oat berries, toss to combine, and season with salt and pepper to taste; set aside.

5   Using highest sauté function, heat remaining 1 tablespoon oil in now-empty pot until just smoking. Add shrimp and cook, tossing constantly, until all but very center is opaque, about 3 minutes.

6   Divide oat berries among individual serving bowls. Top with shrimp, avocado, tortilla chips, and corn salsa. Serve, passing yogurt sauce separately.

Serves 4
Calories 370
Total Time 45 minutes

SHRIMP AND WHITE BEANS
WITH Butternut Squash and Sage

WHY THIS RECIPE WORKS Turning chunks of dense vegetables into tender bites is one of the things an Instant Pot does best. We combined antioxidant-packed butternut squash with fiber-laden cannellini beans for a comforting superfood meal. Sage pairs well with beans, squash, and shrimp separately, but it becomes magical with all three. As well as adding minced sage to the base, we also used the sauté function to produce fried sage leaves for a crispy garnish against the creamy base. Our favored method for shrimp in the Instant Pot is stirring them in raw at the end of cooking and letting the residual heat cook them through. The indirect heat virtually eliminates the chance of overcooking this delicate protein. Extra-large shrimp (21 to 25 per pound) also work in this recipe.

2 tablespoons extra-virgin olive oil, plus extra for drizzling

12 fresh sage leaves, plus 1 tablespoon minced fresh sage

1 onion, chopped fine

4 garlic cloves, minced

½ cup dry white wine

2 (15-ounce) cans cannellini beans, drained with ½ cup canning liquid reserved, rinsed

1½ pounds butternut squash, peeled, seeded, and cut into 1-inch pieces (4 cups)

½ teaspoon table salt

1 pound large shrimp (26 to 30 per pound), peeled, deveined, and tails removed

1 teaspoon grated lemon zest plus 2 teaspoons juice, plus lemon wedges for serving

2 tablespoons toasted sliced almonds

1   Using highest sauté function, cook oil and sage leaves in Instant Pot until sage is dark green and crisp, 3 to 5 minutes, flipping leaves halfway through cooking. Using slotted spoon, transfer sage leaves to paper towel–lined plate.

2   Add onion to oil left in pot and cook until softened and lightly browned, 3 to 5 minutes. Add garlic and minced sage and cook, stirring frequently, until fragrant, about 30 seconds. Stir in wine, scraping up any browned bits, and cook until mostly evaporated, about 1 minute. Stir in beans and reserved liquid, squash, and salt.

3   Lock lid into place and close pressure-release valve. Select high pressure-cook function and cook for 3 minutes. Turn off Instant Pot and quick-release pressure. Carefully remove lid, allowing steam to escape away from you.

4   Stir shrimp gently into squash mixture, cover, and let sit until shrimp are opaque throughout, 5 to 8 minutes. Stir in lemon zest and juice and season with salt and pepper to taste. Sprinkle individual portions with almonds and sage leaves and drizzle with extra oil. Serve with lemon wedges.

SHRIMP JAMBALAYA

1 tablespoon canola oil

1 onion, chopped fine

8 ounces andouille sausage, halved lengthwise and sliced thin

1 green bell pepper, stemmed, seeded, and chopped fine

1 celery rib, minced

5 garlic cloves, minced

1 tablespoon tomato paste

1 teaspoon minced fresh thyme or ¼ teaspoon dried

1 (8-ounce) bottle clam juice

1 cup water

1½ cups long-grain brown rice, rinsed

1 (14.5-ounce) can diced tomatoes, drained with ⅓ cup juice reserved

1 bay leaf

¼ teaspoon table salt

1 pound large shrimp (26 to 30 per pound), peeled, deveined, and tails removed

2 cups frozen cut okra, thawed and patted dry

2 scallions, sliced thin

WHY THIS RECIPE WORKS When it comes to one-pot meals, you can't top shrimp jambalaya. For a Cajun medley of shrimp, sausage, rice, and vegetables, we cooked everything in stages, ensuring optimal flavor and texture in every bite. We started off with onion, green bell pepper, and celery and sweated them with slices of andouille to release its smoky, spicy oil. As a shortcut to deeply flavored seafood broth, we added clam juice instead of chicken broth to cook the brown rice. Tomato paste, diced tomatoes, and reserved tomato juice gave the jambalaya its color and classic flavor. Stirring in the shrimp at the end, off-heat, allowed them to cook through gently. Okra is not always included, but we loved how it bulked up the dish and added a vegetal element. Sprinkling thawed frozen okra over the top allowed it to heat through and arrive at just the right texture as the shrimp cooked. If you can't find andouille sausage, substitute Spanish semicured chorizo, Portuguese chouriço, or linguiça. Extra-large shrimp (21 to 25 per pound) also work in this recipe.

1   Using highest sauté function, heat oil in Instant Pot until shimmering. Add onion, andouille, bell pepper, and celery and cook until vegetables are softened and lightly browned, and andouille is lightly browned, 7 to 9 minutes.

2   Add garlic, tomato paste, and thyme and cook, stirring frequently, until fragrant, about 30 seconds. Stir in clam juice and water, scraping up any browned bits, then stir in rice, tomatoes and reserved juice, bay leaf, and salt. Lock lid into place and close pressure-release valve. Select high pressure-cook function and cook for 25 minutes.

3   Turn off Instant Pot and quick-release pressure. Carefully remove lid, allowing steam to escape away from you. Discard bay leaf. Stir shrimp gently into rice, then arrange okra in even layer on top of rice mixture. Partially cover pot and let sit until shrimp are opaque throughout and okra is heated through, 5 to 8 minutes. Season with salt and pepper to taste. Sprinkle with scallions and serve.

Serves 4 to 6
Calories 350
Total Time 1¼ hours

MUSSELS WITH RED CURRY
AND Coconut Rice

1 tablespoon canola oil

3 tablespoons red curry paste

6 garlic cloves, minced

1½ cups water, divided, plus extra as needed

1 cup canned coconut milk, divided

1 green bell pepper, stemmed, seeded, and cut into 1-inch pieces

1 tomato, cored and cut into ½-inch pieces

2 pounds mussels, scrubbed and debearded

1 teaspoon grated fresh ginger

1 teaspoon grated lime zest, plus lime wedges for serving

1½ cups long-grain brown rice, rinsed

1 tablespoon sugar

½ cup fresh cilantro leaves

WHY THIS RECIPE WORKS Steamed mussels are a quick and healthy meal; they are high in protein yet low in calories and fat. Cooking mussels on the stovetop can be tricky because it's impossible to totally seal the pot and maintain an even temperature, resulting in both overcooked and undercooked mussels. Luckily, the Instant Pot eliminates these problems. We love Thai curries for their sweet and tangy flavors, so jarred red curry paste plus garlic made an amazing base, complementing the briny mussels. Stirring in green pepper and tomato before going under pressure made for a heartier broth. To make creamy brown rice to accompany the mussels, we used a portion of broth along with coconut milk to cook the rice. Discard any raw mussels with an unpleasant odor or with a cracked or broken shell that won't close. To prevent the mussels from overcooking, be sure to turn off the Instant Pot as soon as it reaches pressure.

---

1 Using highest sauté function, heat oil until shimmering. Add curry paste and garlic and cook, stirring frequently, until fragrant, about 30 seconds. Stir in 1 cup water and ½ cup coconut milk, scraping up any browned bits, then stir in bell pepper and tomato. Arrange mussels evenly in pot.

2 Lock lid into place and close pressure-release valve. Select high pressure-cook function and set cook time for 1 minute. Once Instant Pot has reached pressure, immediately turn off pot and quick-release pressure. Carefully remove lid, allowing steam to escape away from you.

3 Transfer mussels to large bowl, discarding any that have not opened. Strain broth through fine-mesh strainer into 2-cup liquid measuring cup (you should have 1½ cups broth; if necessary, add extra water to equal 1½ cups). Stir ginger and lime zest into broth. Transfer solids to bowl with mussels and cover to keep warm.

Serves 4 to 6
Calories 420
Total Time 1¼ hours

4 Return broth to now-empty pot. Stir in rice, sugar, remaining ½ cup water, and remaining ½ cup coconut milk. Lock lid into place and close pressure-release valve. Select high pressure-cook function and cook for 24 minutes. Turn off Instant Pot and quick-release pressure. Carefully remove lid, allowing steam to escape away from you. Fluff rice gently with fork. Lay clean dish towel over pot, replace lid, and let sit for 5 minutes.

5 Divide mussels among individual serving bowls and sprinkle with cilantro leaves. Serve mussels with rice and lime wedges.

CHAPTER 4

VEGETABLES AND GRAINS

133   Hearty Minestrone

134   Green Gumbo

137   Spiced Wild Rice and Coconut Soup

138   Bean and Sweet Potato Chili

140   Green Shakshuka

142   Baba Ghanoush with Chickpea and Arugula Salad

146   Sherry-Braised Leeks on Toast with Red Pepper–Hazelnut Relish

148   Braised Cabbage Wedges with Curry Powder and Chickpeas

151   Black Beans and Brown Rice

152   Chana Masala

155   Braised Lentils and Tofu with Thai Green Curry

156   Braised Tofu with Pumpkin Mole and Apple-Cabbage Slaw

158   Gochujang-Braised Tempeh Lettuce Wraps

160   Farro Salad with Asparagus, Snap Peas, and Tomatoes

162   Smoky Paprika Rice with Crispy Artichokes and Peppers

164   Savory Oatmeal with Sautéed Wild Mushrooms

Serves 6
Calories 270
Total Time 1½ hours, plus 8 hours brining

HEARTY MINESTRONE

WHY THIS RECIPE WORKS Creating anything with fresh flavor in a pressure cooker can be tricky, but we worked to beat the odds and develop a recipe for a lively tasting minestrone that pushes canned soup to the back of the pantry. In creating our minestrone recipe, we tried to squeeze every last ounce of flavor out of a manageable list of supermarket vegetables. Sautéing some of the veggies gave our soup good depth of flavor, while starch from the beans thickened the soup and married a flavorful tomatoey broth with bright vegetables. The last component we considered for our perfect minestrone recipe was the liquid, settling on a combo of vegetable broth, water, and V8 juice (which is an excellent source of vitamins). We added zucchini during the last 5 minutes of cooking to ensure the proper texture, and stirred in fresh basil at the end to enhance the fresh flavors of the soup.

---

1 Dissolve 1½ tablespoons salt in 2 quarts cold water in large container. Add beans and soak at room temperature for at least 8 hours or up to 24 hours. Drain and rinse well.

2 Using highest sauté function, heat 2 tablespoons oil in Instant Pot until shimmering. Add carrots and celery and cook until softened, 5 to 7 minutes. Stir in cabbage, garlic, and pepper flakes and cook until cabbage starts to wilt, about 2 minutes. Stir in beans, 4 cups water, broth, V8 juice, Parmesan rind, if using, and salt.

3 Lock lid into place and close pressure-release valve. Select high pressure-cook function and cook for 30 minutes. Turn off Instant Pot and quick-release pressure. Carefully remove lid, allowing steam to escape away from you.

4 Discard Parmesan rind. Stir in zucchini and cook, using highest sauté function, until tender, about 5 minutes. Stir in basil and remaining 2 tablespoons oil, and season with salt and pepper to taste. Serve, passing extra oil and grated Parmesan separately.

1½ tablespoons table salt for brining

8 ounces (1¼ cups) dried cannellini beans, picked over and rinsed

¼ cup extra-virgin olive oil, divided, plus extra for serving

3 carrots, peeled and cut into ½-inch pieces

3 celery ribs, chopped

4 cups chopped green cabbage

2 garlic cloves, minced

¼ teaspoon red pepper flakes

4 cups vegetable or chicken broth

1½ cups V8 juice

1 Parmesan cheese rind (optional), plus grated Parmesan for serving

1½ teaspoons table salt

2 zucchini, cut into ½-inch pieces

½ cup chopped fresh basil

GREEN GUMBO

1½ tablespoons table salt for brining

8 ounces (1¼ cups) dried black-eyed peas, picked over and rinsed

½ cup canola oil

½ cup all-purpose flour

1 large onion, chopped fine

2 celery ribs, chopped fine

1 green bell pepper, stemmed, seeded, and chopped fine

1 tablespoon minced fresh thyme or 1 teaspoon dried

2 teaspoons table salt

2 teaspoons smoked paprika

¼–½ teaspoon cayenne pepper

12 ounces collard greens, stemmed and chopped

1½ cups frozen cut okra

12 ounces curly-leaf spinach, stemmed and chopped

6 ounces green beans, trimmed and cut into 1-inch lengths

1 tablespoon cider vinegar, plus extra for seasoning

2 scallions, sliced thin

WHY THIS RECIPE WORKS   Green gumbo, originally a Louisiana Lent dish, is set apart from its seafood and meat cousins by greens, and lots of them. A mix of heartier and softer greens gave a nice balance of chew and silkiness. To complement the earthiness of this dish, we amped up the smoky flavor with cayenne and smoked paprika, echoing the taste of gumbos that include smoked meats, but without the saturated fats. Although not traditional, we loved the healthful bulk that added veggies—okra, green beans, and black-eyed peas—brought. A finishing splash of vinegar added a hit of brightness. Kale can be substituted for collards, and Swiss chard can be substituted for spinach. Serve with rice.

1   Dissolve 1½ tablespoons salt in 2 quarts cold water in large container. Add black-eyed peas and soak at room temperature for at least 8 hours or up to 24 hours. Drain and rinse well.

2   Using highest sauté function, heat oil in Instant Pot until shimmering. Add flour and cook, stirring constantly, until mixture is color of milk chocolate, 5 to 10 minutes. Stir in onion, celery, and bell pepper. Cook, stirring frequently, until vegetables have softened, 5 to 8 minutes. Add thyme, salt, paprika, and cayenne and cook, stirring frequently, until fragrant, about 30 seconds.

3   Stir in 5 cups water, scraping up any browned bits and smoothing out any lumps, then stir in black-eyed peas. Arrange collards on top of bean mixture. Lock lid into place and close pressure-release valve. Select high pressure-cook function and cook for 8 minutes.

4   Turn off Instant Pot and quick-release pressure. Carefully remove lid, allowing steam to escape away from you. Stir in okra and, using highest sauté function, bring to simmer. Stir in spinach, 1 handful at a time, and green beans and cook until vegetables are tender, 5 to 7 minutes. Stir in vinegar and season with salt, pepper, and extra vinegar to taste. Sprinkle individual portions with scallions before serving.

Serves 6
Calories 380
Total Time 1¼ hours,
plus 8 hours brining

Serves 6 to 8
Calories 360
Total Time 1¼ hours

SPICED WILD RICE AND COCONUT SOUP

WHY THIS RECIPE WORKS Wild rice can be tricky to cook properly (too little time and it can be hard; too long and it turns gummy), but the Instant Pot turns this grain tender, with just the right amount of chew, in this vibrant, earthy soup. Starting with a sautéed allium base, we added bold garam masala, tomato paste, a serrano chile, and ginger to a combination of vegetable broth and rich coconut milk. We initially put everything in the pot all at once, but the flavors dulled while cooking, so we reserved half of the coconut milk and some ginger to stir in after cooking. For fresh texture, we stirred in Swiss chard until just wilted, letting it maintain its pleasant bite. Some chopped tomato added just the right amount of acid sweetness, and a sprinkle of cilantro provided an herby finish. Do not use quick-cooking or presteamed wild rice (read the ingredients on the package to determine this).

---

1 Using highest sauté function, heat oil in Instant Pot until shimmering. Add onions and chard stems and cook until softened, 3 to 5 minutes. Add garlic, 4 teaspoons ginger, serrano, tomato paste, turmeric, garam masala, and salt and cook, stirring frequently, until fragrant, about 30 seconds. Stir in broth and 1 can coconut milk, scraping up any browned bits, then stir in rice.

2 Lock lid into place and close pressure-release valve. Select high pressure-cook function and cook for 30 minutes. Turn off Instant Pot and quick-release pressure. Carefully remove lid, allowing steam to escape away from you.

3 Stir remaining can coconut milk and chard leaves into soup and cook, using highest sauté function, until chard leaves are wilted, about 5 minutes. Turn off Instant Pot. Stir in remaining 2 teaspoons ginger and tomato and let sit until heated through, about 2 minutes. Stir in cilantro and season with salt and pepper to taste. Serve with lime wedges.

2 tablespoons canola oil

2 onions, chopped fine

8 ounces Swiss chard, stems chopped fine, leaves cut into 1½-inch pieces

6 garlic cloves, minced

2 tablespoons grated fresh ginger, divided

1 serrano chile, stemmed, seeded, and minced

1 tablespoon tomato paste

2 teaspoons ground turmeric

1½ teaspoons garam masala

1½ teaspoons table salt

4 cups vegetable or chicken broth

2 (14-ounce) cans coconut milk, divided

1 cup wild rice, picked over and rinsed

1 tomato, cored and chopped

¼ cup chopped fresh cilantro

Lime wedges

BEAN AND SWEET POTATO CHILI

1½ tablespoons table salt
for brining

1 pound (2½ cups) black,
navy, pinto, and/or small
red beans, rinsed

2 tablespoons ancho chile
powder

1 tablespoon ground coriander

2 teaspoons ground cumin

2 teaspoons dried oregano

1 teaspoon garlic powder

1½ teaspoons table salt

¼ cup extra-virgin olive oil

1 onion, chopped fine

1 (28-ounce) can crushed
tomatoes

2 pounds sweet potatoes,
peeled and cut into 1-inch
pieces

¼ teaspoon baking soda

½ cup chopped fresh cilantro,
divided

Lime wedges

WHY THIS RECIPE WORKS For a familiar chili with a healthful spin, we paired beans with hearty chunks of nutritious sweet potato. To bring classically spiced flavor to our vegetarian version, we bloomed ancho chile powder, coriander, cumin, oregano, and garlic powder in the pot with chopped onion. Adding one can of crushed tomatoes made the perfect base because it broke down into a stewy consistency while maintaining some individual tomato pieces. This dish is so filling and warming that you won't miss the meat. We like a combination of beans, but a single variety will also work well. Diced avocado, yogurt, and shredded Monterey Jack or cheddar cheese are also good options for garnishing.

1 Dissolve 1½ tablespoons salt in 2 quarts cold water in large container. Add beans and soak at room temperature for at least 8 hours or up to 24 hours. Drain and rinse well.

2 Combine chile powder, coriander, cumin, oregano, garlic powder, and salt in bowl. Using highest sauté function, heat oil in Instant Pot until shimmering. Add onion and cook until softened, 3 to 5 minutes. Add spice mixture and cook, stirring frequently, until fragrant, about 30 seconds. Stir in tomatoes and 3 cups water, scraping up any browned bits, then stir in beans, potatoes, and baking soda.

3 Lock lid into place and close pressure-release valve. Select high pressure-cook function and cook for 30 minutes. Turn off Instant Pot and quick-release pressure. Carefully remove lid, allowing steam to escape away from you.

4 Adjust consistency with extra hot water as needed. Stir in ¼ cup cilantro and season with salt and pepper to taste. Sprinkle individual portions with remaining ¼ cup cilantro and serve with lime wedges.

Serves 6 to 8
Calories 400
Total Time 1¼ hours,
plus 8 hours brining

GREEN SHAKSHUKA

1 tablespoon extra-virgin olive oil

2 pounds Swiss chard, stemmed, stems chopped fine to yield 1 cup, leaves chopped

1 onion, chopped

4 garlic cloves, minced

3 tablespoons harissa, divided

⅛ teaspoon table salt

½ cup water

11 ounces (11 cups) baby spinach

1 cup frozen peas

1½ tablespoons lemon juice

4 large eggs

1 ounce feta cheese, crumbled (¼ cup)

¼ cup chopped fresh dill, mint, and/or parsley

WHY THIS RECIPE WORKS Shakshuka is a classic Tunisian one-pot dish with eggs poached in long-simmered spicy tomato sauce. Shakshuka roughly translates to "mixed-up" and can include a mix of vegetables, so we went the green route, with savory Swiss chard, easy-to-prep baby spinach, and tender peas. We started by cooking the Swiss chard stems with onion, then added in garlic and some spicy harissa, to create an aromatic base before putting the Swiss chard leaves under pressure. The Instant Pot wilted the Swiss chard and freed us from the constant stirring needed on the stovetop. To keep the baby spinach from getting gummy and the peas from blowing out in the closed pot, we stirred them in after cooking under pressure. By poaching the eggs directly in the Instant Pot, we kept the recipe as straightforward as possible. For fully set egg whites with runny yolks we cooked the eggs with the high sauté function for 3 minutes and then let them sit in the turned-off pot to finish cooking. A sprinkle of dill and mint gave an herbal finish, and some feta added a tangy contrast. We prefer to make our own Harissa (page 16); however, you can substitute store-bought. Serve with crusty bread.

---

1 Using highest sauté function, heat oil in Instant Pot until shimmering. Add chard stems and onion and cook until softened and lightly browned, about 5 to 7 minutes. Add garlic, 1 tablespoon harissa, and salt and cook, stirring frequently, until fragrant, about 30 seconds. Stir in water, scraping up any browned bits, then arrange chard leaves on top.

2 Lock lid into place and close pressure-release valve. Select high pressure-cook function and cook for 2 minutes. Turn off Instant Pot and quick-release pressure. Carefully remove lid, allowing steam to escape away from you.

3 Stir in spinach, 1 handful at a time, and cook, using highest sauté function, until wilted, about 5 minutes. Stir in peas and lemon juice and season with salt and pepper to taste. Turn off Instant Pot.

Serves 4
Calories 310
Total Time 1 hour

4   Make 4 shallow 2-inch-wide indentations in spinach mixture using back of spoon. Crack 1 egg into each indentation. Spoon spinach and sauce over edges of egg whites so whites are partially covered and yolks are exposed. Using highest sauté function, cook until egg whites are just set, about 3 minutes. Turn off Instant Pot, partially cover pot, and let sit until egg whites are fully set and yolks are still runny, 6 to 10 minutes. Sprinkle individual portions with feta and dill and drizzle with remaining 2 tablespoons harissa before serving.

BABA GHANOUSH
WITH Chickpea and Arugula Salad

2 pounds eggplant, peeled and cut into 2-inch pieces

½ teaspoon table salt, divided

2 tablespoons lemon juice

2 tablespoons tahini

1 tablespoon extra-virgin olive oil

2 garlic cloves, minced

1 (15-ounce) can chickpeas, rinsed

6 ounces cherry tomatoes, halved

2 cups (2 ounces) baby arugula

5 tablespoons Zhoug, divided

½ cup Quick-Pickled Onions (page 19)

4 hard-cooked eggs, halved (page 19)

4 (8-inch) 100 percent whole-wheat pitas, warmed

WHY THIS RECIPE WORKS A plate of creamy baba ghanoush, warm pita bread, and hard-cooked eggs with a tangy chickpea salad is ideal for a light but filling meze-inspired dinner. But baba ghanoush, a Middle Eastern staple of whipped eggplant combined with bright lemon juice, garlic, and nutty tahini, can take over an hour to prepare. It can involve many steps, lots of juggling, sometimes a grill, and often an oven. Traditionally, the eggplant is cooked over a low heat for a long period of time until the center is soft and can be scooped out. This can be a messy process. We discovered that we could cut out multiple steps and much of the mess with the Instant Pot, which streamlined everything and cut our eggplant cook time down to just 6 minutes under pressure—a fraction of the time. By peeling the eggplant before pressure cooking, we were able to eliminate the step of scooping it out. Additionally, the eggplant typically needs to cool completely before being scooped, but by starting with peeled eggplant, the cooling time no longer applied. To cook the eggplant in the pot properly, we needed to add water (to help avoid the dreaded burn notice and to allow the pot to reach pressure), but afterward it was imperative to drain the eggplant for 3 minutes to remove any excess liquid, which could leave the final whipped dish with a bland taste and a thin consistency. The last step was a quick puree in the food processor with the classic additions of lemon juice, tahini, oil, and garlic, which resulted in a silken texture with savory flavor. Zhoug, a spicy cilantro sauce, brightened up our baba ghanoush plate with an herbal punch and did double duty as a dressing for our chickpea salad. While the eggplant cooked, we tossed the chickpeas in a portion of the zhoug, then combined them with bright cherry tomatoes and peppery arugula. Quick-pickled onions brought color and acidity, while the addition of hard-cooked eggs provided extra protein and enough substance for a complete meal.

We prefer to make our own Zhoug (recipe follows); however, you can substitute store-bought, if desired.

1   Combine eggplant, 1 cup water, and ¼ teaspoon salt in Instant Pot. Lock lid into place and close pressure-release valve. Select high pressure-cook function and cook for 6 minutes. Turn off Instant Pot and quick-release pressure. Carefully remove lid, allowing steam to escape away from you.

2   Transfer eggplant to colander set over bowl and let drain for 3 minutes; discard cooking liquid. Pulse eggplant, lemon juice, tahini, oil, garlic, and remaining ¼ teaspoon salt in food processor to coarse puree, about 8 pulses, scraping down sides of bowl as needed. Season with salt and pepper to taste.

3   Toss chickpeas, tomatoes, and arugula with 2 tablespoons zhoug in bowl. Season with salt and pepper to taste. Spread portion of baba ghanoush over bottom of individual serving plates and drizzle with remaining 3 tablespoons zhoug. Arrange chickpea salad, pickled onions, and eggs on top. Serve with pita.

ZHOUG
Makes about ½ cup
Zhoug is an Israeli hot sauce that can be either red or green; it can add instant spice to grain bowls, soups, or anything else you like.

- 6   tablespoons extra-virgin olive oil
- ½   teaspoon ground coriander
- ¼   teaspoon ground cumin
- ¼   teaspoon ground cardamom
- ¼   teaspoon table salt
  Pinch ground cloves
- ¾   cup fresh cilantro leaves
- ½   cup fresh parsley leaves
- 2   green Thai chiles, stemmed and chopped
- 2   garlic cloves, minced

1   Microwave oil, coriander, cumin, cardamom, salt, and cloves in covered bowl until fragrant, about 30 seconds; let cool to room temperature.

2   Pulse oil-spice mixture, cilantro, parsley, chiles, and garlic in food processor until coarse paste forms, about 15 pulses, scraping down sides of bowl as needed. (Zhoug can be refrigerated for up to 4 days.)

photo on following page >

Baba Ghanoush with Chickpea and
Arugula Salad, page 142

SHERRY-BRAISED LEEKS ON TOAST
WITH Red Pepper–Hazelnut Relish

½ cup jarred roasted red peppers, rinsed, patted dry, and chopped fine

¼ cup hazelnuts, toasted, skinned, and chopped

¼ cup extra-virgin olive oil, divided

2 tablespoons chopped fresh parsley

1 teaspoon sherry vinegar

1 small garlic clove, minced

1 teaspoon table salt, divided

4 leeks, trimmed to bottom 6 inches, halved lengthwise, and washed thoroughly

2 sprigs fresh rosemary

⅓ cup dry sherry

⅔ cup water

3 ounces (¾ cup) goat cheese, softened

4 (½-inch-thick) slices rustic 100 percent whole-grain bread, toasted

WHY THIS RECIPE WORKS In Catalonia there is a famed dish of grilled calçots (a type of local spring onion) served with a loose romesco—a sauce made of pounded almonds, garlic, peppers, oil, and vinegar. Here, halved leeks stood in for the calçots, and we used the Instant Pot's powerful sauté function to char them. We then braised the leeks in sherry and rosemary until meltingly tender and sweet. Not wanting to waste the flavorful liquid, we whisked in some goat cheese to turn it into a glossy, tangy emulsion and slathered it over toast. We topped it off with a hazelnut roasted pepper relish, which gave us the flavor of romesco without the knife work or the need to pull out a food processor. Look for leeks that are 1 to 1¼ inches in diameter at the base. If using larger leeks, peel away outer layers to achieve the correct size.

---

1 Combine red peppers, hazelnuts, 2 tablespoons oil, parsley, vinegar, garlic, and ¼ teaspoon salt in bowl; set aside for serving. (Relish can be refrigerated for up to 2 days; bring to room temperature and stir to recombine before serving.)

2 Pat leeks dry with paper towels. Using highest sauté function, heat 1 tablespoon oil in Instant Pot until just smoking. Arrange half of leeks cut side down in single layer in pot. Cook, pressing gently on leeks with spatula to create good contact between leeks and pot, until well browned on first side, 4 to 6 minutes. Transfer leeks to plate, taking care to keep layers intact. Repeat with remaining 1 tablespoon oil and remaining leeks; transfer to plate. Turn off Instant Pot.

3 Add rosemary sprigs to oil left in pot and cook, using residual heat, until fragrant, about 30 seconds. Stir in sherry, scraping up any browned bits, then stir in water and ½ teaspoon salt. Arrange leeks cut side up in pot in even layer (leeks may overlap). Lock lid into place and close pressure-release valve. Select high pressure-cook function and cook for 5 minutes.

Serves 4
Calories 370
Total Time 45 minutes

4 Turn off Instant Pot and quick-release pressure. Carefully remove lid, allowing steam to escape away from you. Discard rosemary sprigs. Transfer leeks carefully to plate and sprinkle with remaining ¼ teaspoon salt. Whisk ¼ cup braising liquid and goat cheese together in bowl until completely smooth. Spread goat cheese mixture evenly on toast and arrange on individual plates. Top with leeks and relish. Serve.

BRAISED CABBAGE WEDGES
WITH Curry Powder and Chickpeas

½ cup plain whole-milk yogurt

6 tablespoons chopped fresh cilantro, divided

3 garlic cloves, minced, divided

¼ teaspoon grated lime zest plus 1 teaspoon juice

1 head green cabbage (2 pounds)

¼ cup canola oil, divided

1 tablespoon curry powder

2 teaspoons grated fresh ginger

1 (14.5-ounce) can diced tomatoes

½ cup water

¼ teaspoon table salt

2 (15-ounce) cans chickpeas, rinsed

¼ cup slivered almonds, toasted

WHY THIS RECIPE WORKS Rather than cabbage playing a bit part to corned beef or being used as fodder for coleslaw, we wanted to thrust it firmly to center stage. We love cabbage for its ability to take on browning and to turn startling sweet and tender inside when braised. Using the Instant Pot's intense sauté function, we found that the cabbage was equally flavorful when we achieved deep browning on just one side, which cut down on time and meant we didn't need to execute an awkward flip in the pot. We bloomed curry powder and ginger in the residual oil and added diced tomatoes and chickpeas to make a hearty accompaniment in which to braise the seared wedges. A cilantro-lime yogurt dressing pulled the components together, and slivered almonds offered a pleasantly contrasting crunch.

---

1   Combine yogurt, 2 tablespoons cilantro, ¼ teaspoon garlic, and lime zest and juice in bowl. Season with salt and pepper to taste; set aside for serving.

2   Halve cabbage through core and cut each half into 4 even wedges, leaving core intact. Using highest sauté function, heat 2 tablespoons oil in Instant Pot until just smoking. Arrange 4 cabbage wedges cut side down in single layer in pot. Cook, pressing gently on cabbage with spatula to create good contact between cabbage and pot, until well browned on first side, 5 to 7 minutes. Transfer cabbage to plate. Repeat with remaining 4 wedges and remaining 2 tablespoons oil. Turn off Instant Pot.

3   Add curry powder, ginger, and remaining garlic to oil left in pot and cook, using residual heat, stirring frequently, until fragrant, about 30 seconds. Stir in tomatoes and their juice, water, and salt, scraping up any browned bits. Reserve 1 cup tomato mixture, then stir chickpeas into pot. Nestle cabbage wedges browned side up

Serves 4
Calories 400
Total Time 1 hour

into chickpea mixture (wedges will overlap) and spoon reserved tomato mixture over tops. Lock lid into place and close pressure-release valve. Select high pressure-cook function and cook for 4 minutes.

4   Turn off Instant Pot and quick-release pressure. Carefully remove lid, allowing steam to escape away from you. Divide cabbage among individual plates. Season chickpea mixture with salt and pepper to taste and spoon over cabbage. Sprinkle with almonds and remaining ¼ cup cilantro. Serve with yogurt sauce.

BLACK BEANS AND BROWN RICE

WHY THIS RECIPE WORKS Beans and rice is a classic one-pot comfort food the world over. But stovetop recipes can sometimes lead to blown-out rice and undercooked beans, or vice versa. Luckily, the Instant Pot can be calibrated with just the right amount of liquid and time to produce fluffy rice and tender beans consistently. We chose brown rice for its high fiber content and hearty texture. The beans are the stars of this meal, so we picked dried over canned for their superior taste and texture. As they cooked, they imparted flavor and color into the rice while maintaining structural integrity. For a savory base, we started by sautéing bell peppers, onions, and jalapeños, adding in garlic, oregano, cumin, and tomato paste. After adding the broth and cooking everything for 22 minutes, we had a warm, perfect pot of rice and beans. We finished this deceptively simple but flavor-packed dish with scallions and a splash of red wine vinegar. Do not substitute white rice here.

---

1   Dissolve 1½ tablespoons salt in 2 quarts cold water in large container. Add beans and soak at room temperature for at least 8 hours or up to 24 hours. Drain and rinse well.

2   Using highest sauté function, heat oil in Instant Pot until shimmering. Add bell peppers, onion, and jalapeños and cook until vegetables are softened and lightly browned, 5 to 7 minutes. Add garlic, tomato paste, oregano, cumin, and salt and cook, stirring frequently, until fragrant, about 30 seconds. Stir in broth, scraping up any browned bits, then stir in beans and rice.

3   Lock lid into place and close pressure-release valve. Select high pressure-cook function and cook for 22 minutes. Turn off Instant Pot and quick-release pressure. Carefully remove lid, allowing steam to escape away from you.

4   Lay clean dish towel over pot, replace lid, and let sit for 5 minutes. Sprinkle scallions and vinegar over rice and beans and fluff gently with fork to combine. Season with salt and pepper to taste. Serve with lime wedges.

1½   tablespoons table salt for brining

8   ounces (1¼ cups) dried black beans, picked over and rinsed

1   tablespoon canola oil

2   green bell peppers, stemmed, seeded, and chopped fine

1   onion, chopped fine

2   jalapeño chiles, stemmed, seeded, and minced

6   garlic cloves, minced

1   tablespoon tomato paste

2   teaspoons dried oregano

2   teaspoons ground cumin

1¼   teaspoons table salt

2¾   cups vegetable broth

1½   cups long-grain brown rice, rinsed

4   scallions, sliced thin

2   tablespoons red wine vinegar

   Lime wedges

CHANA MASALA

1½ tablespoons table salt for brining

8 ounces (1¼ cups) dried chickpeas, picked over and rinsed

1 small red onion, three-quarters chopped coarse, one-quarter chopped fine

10 sprigs fresh cilantro, stems and leaves separated, stems cut into 1-inch lengths

1 (1½-inch) piece ginger, peeled and chopped coarse

2 garlic cloves, chopped coarse

2 serrano chiles, stemmed, halved, seeded, and sliced thin crosswise, divided

1 (14.5-ounce) can whole peeled tomatoes

3 tablespoons canola oil

1 teaspoon paprika

1 teaspoon ground cumin

1 teaspoon table salt

½ teaspoon ground turmeric

½ teaspoon fennel seeds

1½ teaspoons garam masala

WHY THIS RECIPE WORKS Chana masala is one of northern India's most popular vegetarian dishes, and it can be quick and easy to prepare, especially in the Instant Pot. We started by using the food processor to finely chop the aromatics that formed the base of our dish. A combination of water and processed whole canned tomatoes provided enough liquid to cook the chickpeas, and after 20 minutes under pressure they were perfectly tender. As an added benefit, the starches released by the chickpeas while cooking added body and savory depth to the dish. Using stronger foundational spices such as cumin, turmeric, and fennel seeds at the beginning of cooking ensured that they permeated the dish while cooking, and reserving the sweet, delicate garam masala until near the end preserved its aroma. A generous garnish of chopped onion, sliced chile, and cilantro added so much vibrancy, texture, and freshness that you'd never guess that most of the ingredients in the recipe were from the pantry. Serve with rice, naan, and/or lime wedges.

---

1 Dissolve 1½ tablespoons salt in 2 quarts cold water in large container. Add chickpeas and soak at room temperature for at least 8 hours or up to 24 hours. Drain and rinse well.

2 Process coarsely chopped onion, cilantro stems, ginger, garlic, and half of serranos in food processor until finely chopped, scraping down sides of bowl as necessary, about 20 seconds; transfer to bowl. Process tomatoes and their juice in now-empty processor until smooth, about 30 seconds.

3 Using highest sauté function, heat oil in Instant Pot until shimmering. Add onion mixture and cook until softened and lightly browned, 3 to 5 minutes. Add paprika, cumin, salt, turmeric, and fennel seeds and cook, stirring frequently, until fragrant, about 30 seconds. Stir in 3 cups water, chickpeas, and processed tomatoes.

Serves 4
Calories 270
Total Time 1¼ hours, plus 8 hours brining

4 Lock lid into place and close pressure-release valve. Select high pressure-cook function and cook for 20 minutes. Turn off Instant Pot and quick-release pressure. Carefully remove lid, allowing steam to escape away from you.

5 Stir garam masala into chickpea mixture and continue to cook, using highest sauté function, until sauce is thickened, 8 to 12 minutes. Season chickpea mixture with salt to taste. Transfer to wide, shallow serving bowl. Sprinkle with finely chopped onion, remaining serranos, and cilantro leaves. Serve.

Serves 4
Calories 310
Total Time 1 hour

BRAISED LENTILS AND TOFU
WITH Thai Green Curry

WHY THIS RECIPE WORKS Thai curries embrace a balance of textures and colors to produce lively meals packed with veggies and protein. For a Thai-influenced green curry that was full of flavor, we started by cooking fiber-rich lentils in an aromatic green curry broth. Thanks to the even cooking of the Instant Pot, the lentils kept their texture while absorbing flavorful liquid. Once they were cooked, we stirred in coconut milk to create a rich, creamy sauce. Red bell pepper and snow peas contrasted the earthiness of the lentils and gave a pop of color, while cubed tofu provided additional protein. Using the sauté function, we warmed the dish through so the vegetables could maintain their color and crisp texture. A handful of basil stirred in at the end gave a heady finish. Do not substitute green or brown lentils for the lentilles du Puy (also known as French green lentils).

---

1 Spread tofu on paper towel–lined baking sheet, let drain for 20 minutes, then gently press dry with paper towels. Sprinkle with salt and pepper.

2 Meanwhile, whisk water and curry paste together in Instant Pot, then stir in lentils and salt. Lock lid into place and close pressure-release valve. Select high pressure-cook function and cook for 16 minutes. Turn off Instant Pot and quick-release pressure. Carefully remove lid, allowing steam to escape away from you.

3 Stir coconut milk and fish sauce into lentils and bring to simmer using highest sauté function. Stir in tofu, bell pepper, and snow peas, partially cover pot, and cook, stirring occasionally, until tofu is heated through and vegetables are crisp-tender, about 3 minutes. Turn off Instant Pot.

4 Stir in basil and lime juice. Season with salt, pepper, and fish sauce to taste. Sprinkle individual portions with scallions. Serve with lime wedges.

14 ounces extra-firm tofu, cut into ½-inch pieces

2 cups water

3 tablespoons Thai green curry paste

1 cup dried lentilles du Puy, picked over and rinsed

¾ teaspoon table salt

½ cup canned coconut milk

1 tablespoon fish sauce, plus extra for seasoning

1 red bell pepper, stemmed, seeded, and cut into ¼-inch-wide strips

4 ounces snow peas, strings removed and halved crosswise

½ cup coarsely chopped fresh Thai or Italian basil

1 tablespoon lime juice, plus lime wedges for serving

2 scallions, sliced thin

BRAISED TOFU
WITH Pumpkin Mole and Apple-Cabbage Slaw

¼ cup cider vinegar

1 tablespoon sugar

¾ teaspoon table salt, divided

2 cups shredded red cabbage

1 shallot, sliced thin

½ cup golden raisins, divided

1 Granny Smith apple, cored and cut into matchsticks

1 (14.5-ounce) can fire-roasted diced tomatoes

6 garlic cloves, minced

1½ tablespoons unsweetened cocoa powder

1 tablespoon minced canned chipotle chile in adobo sauce

1 teaspoon ground cinnamon

2 cups water

1 (14-ounce) block firm tofu, quartered

1 (15-ounce) can unsweetened pumpkin puree

2 ounces cotija cheese, crumbled (½ cup)

WHY THIS RECIPE WORKS We know the Instant Pot creates beautifully braised meat dishes, and for a filling vegetarian meal we wanted to apply the same method to a block of tofu. Tofu is a perfect blank canvas, and when braised it readily soaks up all the flavorful liquid to become tender and creamy. We combined fire-roasted tomatoes, chipotle chiles in adobo, garlic, golden raisins, and cocoa powder for a mole-inspired sauce. To ensure the tofu absorbed maximum flavor but still kept its shape, we cut it into quarters before nestling it into the sauce. After cooking, we removed the tofu from the liquid and whisked in pumpkin puree. Its natural sweetness and mellow squash notes balanced the smoky flavors and enhanced the luscious, velvety sauce, which we then spooned over the tofu. An easy slaw of cabbage, apple, shallots, and more golden raisins made for a tart, crunchy sidekick to the tofu. We love serving this with brown rice (pages 8-9) and tortillas for a heartier meal and for sopping up all the delicious sauce.

---

1 Microwave vinegar, sugar, and ¼ teaspoon salt in large bowl until steaming, 1 to 2 minutes; whisk to dissolve sugar and salt. Add cabbage, shallot, and ¼ cup raisins to hot brine and let sit, stirring occasionally, for 30 minutes. Drain cabbage mixture and return to now-empty bowl. Stir in apple and set aside for serving. (Slaw can be refrigerated for up to 24 hours.)

2 Meanwhile, process tomatoes and their juice, garlic, cocoa powder, chipotle, cinnamon, remaining ½ teaspoon salt, and remaining ¼ cup raisins in food processor until smooth, 1 to 2 minutes, scraping down sides of bowl as needed. Whisk tomato mixture and water together in Instant Pot. Arrange tofu in even layer in pot and spoon some of sauce over top. Lock lid into place and close pressure-release valve. Select high pressure-cook function and cook for 5 minutes.

Serves 4
Calories 320
Total Time 1 hour

3 Turn off Instant Pot and quick-release pressure. Carefully remove lid, allowing steam to escape away from you. Transfer tofu to serving dish and tent with aluminum foil. Whisk pumpkin into sauce and cook, using highest sauté function, whisking constantly, until sauce is slightly thickened, 2 to 3 minutes. Season with salt and pepper to taste. Spoon sauce over tofu and sprinkle with cotija. Serve tofu with apple-cabbage slaw.

GOCHUJANG-BRAISED TEMPEH LETTUCE WRAPS

1 cup unseasoned rice vinegar

2 tablespoons sugar

1 cucumber, peeled, quartered lengthwise, seeded, and sliced thin on bias

4 ounces (2 cups) bean sprouts

4 scallions, sliced thin

4 teaspoons toasted sesame oil, divided

4 teaspoons grated fresh ginger, divided

1 cup water

3 tablespoons gochujang paste

2 tablespoons honey

2 tablespoons soy sauce, plus extra for seasoning

4 garlic cloves, minced

1 pound tempeh, halved lengthwise and cut crosswise into ½-inch pieces

1 tablespoon sesame seeds, toasted

2 heads Bibb lettuce (8 ounces each), leaves separated

WHY THIS RECIPE WORKS For a meal that is fun to eat and easy to make, we turned to lettuce wrapped around sweet, savory tempeh and crisp pickled vegetables. We wanted a vegetarian lettuce cup filling that was just as satisfying as its meaty counterparts. Tempeh, made from fermented soybeans, is high in protein, fiber, and probiotics and has a nutty flavor with a meaty chew, making it the perfect choice. For a sauce that was sweet and spicy we whisked together gochujang (Korean red pepper paste), honey, soy sauce, sesame oil, ginger, and garlic. Cooking in the Instant Pot allowed the tempeh to soften slightly and soak up the flavorful sauce without drying out. Once the tempeh was done, we removed it from the pot and reduced the sauce on high. Crunchy pickles offset the spicy tempeh for a refreshing dinner with a kick.

---

1 Microwave vinegar and sugar in medium bowl until steaming, 1 to 2 minutes; whisk to dissolve sugar. Add cucumber and bean sprouts to hot brine and let sit, stirring occasionally, for 30 minutes. Drain cucumber mixture and return to now-empty bowl. Stir in scallions, 1 teaspoon oil, and 1 teaspoon ginger; set aside for serving. (Pickled vegetables can be refrigerated for up to 24 hours.)

2 Meanwhile, whisk water, gochujang, honey, soy sauce, garlic, remaining 1 tablespoon oil, and remaining 1 tablespoon ginger together in Instant Pot. Arrange tempeh in even layer in pot and spoon sauce over top. Lock lid into place and close pressure-release valve. Select high pressure-cook function and cook for 12 minutes.

3 Turn off Instant Pot and quick-release pressure. Carefully remove lid, allowing steam to escape away from you. Transfer tempeh to serving dish. Using highest sauté function, cook sauce, stirring occasionally, until slightly thickened, 1 to 2 minutes. Season with extra soy sauce to taste. Spoon sauce over tempeh and sprinkle with sesame seeds. Serve in lettuce leaves with pickled vegetables.

Serves 4
Calories 380
Total Time 45 minutes

FARRO SALAD

WITH Asparagus, Snap Peas, and Tomatoes

1½ cups whole farro

¼ cup extra-virgin olive oil, divided

¼ teaspoon salt, plus salt for cooking farro

6 ounces asparagus, trimmed and cut into 1-inch lengths

6 ounces sugar snap peas, strings removed and cut into 1-inch lengths

2 tablespoons lemon juice

2 tablespoons minced shallot

1 teaspoon Dijon mustard

¼ teaspoon pepper

6 ounces cherry tomatoes, halved

3 tablespoons chopped fresh dill, basil, and/or parsley

2 ounces feta cheese, crumbled (½ cup), divided

WHY THIS RECIPE WORKS Since the Instant Pot is a convenient way to cook your favorite whole grains, we decided to highlight this with a hearty farro salad. Our experience cooking rice and grains in the Instant Pot taught us the importance of using enough water for even cooking, adding a little oil to reduce starchy foam, and letting the pressure release naturally after cooking. The farro cooked so quickly under pressure that we found it was best to turn off the Instant Pot as soon as it came to pressure and let the cooking take place while it depressurized for 15 minutes. To make sure this salad looked as good as it tasted, we briefly blanched bite-size pieces of asparagus and snap peas in the hot cooking liquid before draining the farro. This brought out their vibrant color and crisp-tender bite. A lemon-herb dressing served as a complement to the earthy farro, while cherry tomatoes and feta cheese offered a fresh, full-flavored finish. Do not use quick-cooking or presteamed farro in this recipe.

---

1 Combine 6 cups water, farro, 1 tablespoon oil, and 1½ teaspoons salt in Instant Pot. Lock lid into place and close pressure-release valve. Select high pressure-cook function and set cook time for 1 minute. Once Instant Pot has reached pressure, immediately turn off pot and let pressure release naturally for 15 minutes. Quick-release any remaining pressure, then carefully remove lid, allowing steam to escape away from you.

2 Stir asparagus and snap peas into pot and let sit until crisp-tender, about 3 minutes. Drain farro and vegetables, rinse with cold water, and drain again.

3 Whisk remaining 3 tablespoons oil, salt, lemon juice, shallot, mustard, and pepper together in large bowl. Add farro and vegetables, tomatoes, dill, and ¼ cup feta and toss gently to combine. Season with salt and pepper to taste. Transfer to serving platter and sprinkle with remaining ¼ cup feta. Serve.

Serves 4 to 6
Calories 290
Total Time 1 hour

SMOKY PAPRIKA RICE
WITH Crispy Artichokes and Peppers

¼ cup extra-virgin olive oil, divided

2 cups jarred whole baby artichokes packed in water, rinsed, halved, and patted dry

2 red bell peppers, stemmed, seeded, and cut into ½-inch-wide strips

1 onion, chopped fine

2 cups Arborio rice

6 garlic cloves, minced

2 tablespoons tomato paste

1 teaspoon smoked paprika

Pinch saffron threads, crumbled

½ cup dry white wine

2 cups vegetable broth

2 cups water

1 (14.5-ounce) can fire-roasted diced tomatoes, drained

¾ teaspoon table salt

½ cup pitted kalamata olives, halved

½ cup frozen peas, thawed

1 tablespoon lemon juice, plus lemon wedges for serving

3 tablespoons chopped fresh parsley

WHY THIS RECIPE WORKS We wanted to make a hearty vegetarian recipe that was heavily inspired by paella, the saffron-infused rice dish from Valencia, minus the eponymous pan over an outdoor fire. Paella often has a couple of "hero" ingredients, such as smoky sausage or seafood, to boost its flavor, and we wanted to take the same approach but with plants. Artichokes are a traditional addition, and we found that by first carefully searing jarred artichokes we could achieve a stunning, golden-brown main component. Fire-roasted tomatoes added further smoky notes, while olives and tomato paste offered concentrated umami. Short-grain Arborio rice gave us a satisfyingly chewy texture and cooked in just 1 minute under pressure, making this show-stopping dish a weeknight-friendly one too.

---

1   Using highest sauté function, heat 1 tablespoon oil in Instant Pot until just smoking. Arrange half of artichokes cut side down in single layer in pot. Cook, pressing gently on artichokes with spatula to create good contact between artichokes and pot, until well browned on first side, 3 to 5 minutes; transfer to plate. Repeat with 1 tablespoon oil and remaining artichokes; transfer to plate.

2   Add bell peppers, onion, and remaining 2 tablespoons oil to fat left in pot and cook, using highest sauté function, until vegetables are softened and lightly browned, 7 to 10 minutes. Add rice, garlic, tomato paste, paprika, and saffron and cook, stirring frequently, until fragrant, about 1 minute. Stir in wine, scraping up any browned bits, then stir in broth, water, tomatoes, and salt.

3   Lock lid into place and close pressure-release valve. Select high pressure-cook function and cook for 1 minute. Turn off Instant Pot and quick-release pressure. Carefully remove lid, allowing steam to escape away from you.

4 Stir olives, peas, and half of artichokes into rice mixture, cover, and let sit for 5 minutes. Stir in lemon juice and season with salt and pepper to taste. Arrange remaining artichokes on top of rice mixture and sprinkle with parsley. Serve with lemon wedges.

SAVORY OATMEAL
WITH Sautéed Wild Mushrooms

5 tablespoons extra-virgin olive oil, divided, plus extra for drizzling

1 pound leeks, trimmed, halved lengthwise, sliced thin, and washed and dried thoroughly, divided

1 pound cremini, chanterelle, shiitake, and/or oyster mushroom, stemmed and cut or torn into 1½-inch pieces

½ teaspoon table salt, divided

1 teaspoon minced fresh thyme

1½ cups steel-cut oats

½ cup dry white wine

4½ cups water, plus extra as needed

3 ounces ricotta salata, shredded (¾ cup), plus extra for serving

½ cup chopped fresh parsley, plus extra leaves for serving

1 tablespoon lemon juice

WHY THIS RECIPE WORKS We've had great success cooking risottos, farrottos, pilafs, and polentas in the Instant Pot, so it didn't require a stretch of the imagination to conclude that a savory oatmeal would be exceptionally easy and delicious. To make this a rounded meal, we bulked up the base by softening almost a pound of leeks. After softening steel-cut oats to eke out that extra-toasty flavor, we deglazed with wine and cooked under pressure. This yielded a super-creamy porridge, as the starches in the oats gelled into a thick, comforting consistency without the need to add butter or cream. Mushrooms, garlic, and thyme are a classic combination and worked well just being seared and stirred in at the end. Wanting a little extra texture, we sautéed a portion of the sliced leeks until golden brown, and we loved these sweet, crispy strands with the savory mushrooms and satisfying porridge.

---

1 Using highest sauté function, heat 2 tablespoons oil in Instant Pot until shimmering. Add ¼ cup leeks and cook, stirring often, until beginning to brown, 2 to 3 minutes. Turn off Instant Pot and continue to cook, using residual heat, until leeks are evenly golden brown and crisp, 2 to 3 minutes. Using slotted spoon, transfer leeks to paper towel-lined bowl; set aside.

2 Add mushrooms and ¼ teaspoon salt to fat left in pot. Partially cover and cook, using highest sauté function, stirring occasionally, until mushrooms release their liquid, about 5 minutes. Uncover and continue to cook until liquid has evaporated and mushrooms begin to brown, 8 to 10 minutes. Add thyme and cook, stirring frequently, until fragrant, about 30 seconds; transfer to separate bowl.

3 Add remaining leeks and 1 tablespoon oil to now-empty pot and cook, using highest sauté function, until leeks are softened, 3 to 5 minutes. Stir in oats and cook until fragrant, about 2 minutes. Stir in wine and cook until nearly evaporated, about 30 seconds.

Serves 4
Calories 560
Total Time 1¼ hours

Stir in water and remaining ¼ teaspoon salt, scraping up any browned bits. Lock lid into place and close pressure-release valve. Select high pressure-cook function and cook for 10 minutes.

4 Turn off Instant Pot and quick-release pressure. Partially uncover with care, allowing steam to escape away from you, and let sit for 5 minutes. Add ricotta salata and remaining 2 tablespoons

oil and stir vigorously until oatmeal becomes creamy. Adjust consistency with extra hot water as needed. Stir in parsley, lemon juice, and half of mushrooms. Season with salt and pepper to taste.

5 Divide oatmeal among individual serving bowls. Top with remaining mushrooms, reserved leeks, extra ricotta salata, and extra parsley leaves. Drizzle with extra oil before serving.

CHAPTER 5

PASTA AND NOODLES

168   Spaghetti and Turkey Meatballs

170   Parmesan Penne with Chicken and Asparagus

174   Fusilli with Braised Pork, Fennel, and Lemon

176   Spaghetti with Mushrooms, Kale, and Fontina

179   Creamy Spring Vegetable Linguine

180   Rigatoni with Mushroom Ragù

182   Shells with Butternut Squash, Leeks, and Burrata

184   Fideos with Chickpeas, Fennel, and Spinach

186   Sopa Seca with Chorizo and Black Beans

188   Sweet and Savory Rice Noodles with Chicken and Green Beans

191   Ginger Ramen Noodles with Beef and Bok Choy

192   Sweet Potato Glass Noodles with Portobellos and Spinach

SPAGHETTI AND TURKEY MEATBALLS

1 pound 100 percent whole-wheat spaghetti

1 ounce Parmesan cheese, grated (½ cup), plus extra for serving

¼ cup panko bread crumbs

3 tablespoons plus ¼ cup chopped fresh basil, divided

1 large egg

6 garlic cloves, minced, divided

¾ teaspoon table salt, divided

1 pound ground turkey

2 tablespoons extra-virgin olive oil

2 tablespoons minced fresh oregano or 2 teaspoons dried

1 tablespoon tomato paste

1 (28-ounce) can crushed tomatoes

2 cups chicken or vegetable broth

2 cups water

WHY THIS RECIPE WORKS Spaghetti and meatballs is the ultimate comfort food, but it is often axed in the name of eating healthy. With a few adjustments and the Instant Pot, we were able to deliver a mess-free, healthier version that still satisfies the soul. For our meatballs, instead of beef or pork, we used lighter ground turkey mixed with Parmesan, fresh basil, and an egg for moisture. To infuse our dish with familiar flavor, we began by blooming oregano, tomato paste, and garlic using the high sauté function. One can of crushed tomatoes, along with broth and water, provided the right amount of liquid to cook our whole-wheat pasta and meatballs under pressure. Breaking the pasta into 6-inch lengths helped ensure all noodles were fully submerged for even cooking. Be sure to use ground turkey, not ground turkey breast (also labeled 99 percent fat-free). You can substitute traditional spaghetti for the whole-wheat. Do not substitute other pasta shapes.

---

1   Loosely wrap half of pasta in dish towel, then press bundle against corner of counter to break noodles into 6-inch lengths; repeat with remaining pasta. Set aside.

2   Combine Parmesan, panko, 3 tablespoons basil, egg, half of garlic, and ¼ teaspoon salt in large bowl. Add turkey and knead with hands until thoroughly combined. Pinch off and roll mixture into twelve 1½-inch meatballs.

3   Using highest sauté function, heat oil in Instant Pot until shimmering. Add oregano, tomato paste, and remaining garlic and cook, stirring frequently, until fragrant, about 30 seconds. Stir in tomatoes, broth, water, and remaining ½ teaspoon salt, scraping up any browned bits. Nestle meatballs into sauce, then arrange pasta in even layer on top of meatballs.

4   Lock lid into place and close pressure-release valve. Select high pressure-cook function and cook for 6 minutes. Turn off Instant Pot and quick-release pressure. Carefully remove lid, allowing steam to escape away from you.

Serves 4 to 6
Calories 460
Total Time 1 hour

5 Gently stir spaghetti, meatballs, and sauce to combine. Partially cover pot and let sit until spaghetti is tender and sauce is thickened, 5 to 8 minutes. Stir in remaining ¼ cup basil and season with salt and pepper to taste. Serve, passing extra Parmesan separately.

PARMESAN PENNE
WITH Chicken and Asparagus

10 garlic cloves, minced

2 tablespoons extra-virgin olive oil

1/8–1/4 teaspoon red pepper flakes

1/2 cup dry white wine

4 cups chicken broth

1 cup water

1 pound 100 percent whole-wheat penne

3/4 teaspoon table salt

2 (6- to 8-ounce) boneless, skinless chicken breasts, trimmed and halved lengthwise

1 pound asparagus, trimmed and sliced 1/4 inch thick on bias

10 ounces cherry tomatoes, halved

2 ounces Parmesan cheese, grated (1 cup), plus extra for serving

1/4 cup chopped fresh basil, plus extra for serving

WHY THIS RECIPE WORKS One-pot pasta dishes in the Instant Pot provoked a sort of epiphany for us: In a few simple steps and mere minutes under pressure, we could achieve a balanced combination of al dente pasta, velvety sauce, and tender vegetables with flavorful proteins. Although one-pot pasta dishes are achievable on the stovetop, we came up with a foolproof method with the Instant Pot that enabled us to bang out winner after winner in a fraction of the time. Why would we ever go back to the boil-and-drain method again? Granted, cooking pasta under pressure means it's impossible to check for doneness partway through cooking, so one could worry that what you gain in speed you lose in accuracy. After cooking our way through dozens of pastas while cross-checking cook times across Instant Pot models, we discovered that the key was to slightly undercook the pasta under pressure. Then, using a combination of the sauté function and residual heat (depending on the recipe), we simmered or rested the contents of the pot until the pasta and any additional proteins or vegetables were completely cooked and the sauce had achieved a perfect texture. Using this approach, we wanted to attempt a classic crowd-pleasing dish that combined whole-wheat penne pasta in a garlicky Parmesan sauce with chicken breasts, asparagus, tomatoes, and fresh basil. We started by creating a potent base using a generous amount of lightly toasted garlic in olive oil, plus some pepper flakes and a splash of white wine. After testing our way through the ideal cook times for the pasta and the chicken, we found that we could cook both together, which further enhanced the flavors of the pasta as it simmered in the flavorful chicken liquid. After turning off the pot and releasing pressure, we removed and shredded the chicken; meanwhile, we stirred sliced asparagus and tomatoes into the pasta and used the high sauté function to soften and warm the vegetables through while thickening the pasta sauce. To finish the dish, we added the shredded chicken back in along with generous helpings of Parmesan cheese and fresh basil.

1 Using highest sauté function, cook garlic, oil, and pepper flakes in Instant Pot until fragrant, about 3 minutes. Stir in wine, scraping up any browned bits, and cook until mostly evaporated, about 1 minute. Stir in broth, water, pasta, and salt, then nestle chicken into pasta mixture.

2 Lock lid into place and close pressure-release valve. Select high pressure-cook function and cook for 4 minutes. Turn off Instant Pot and quick-release pressure. Carefully remove lid, allowing steam to escape away from you. Transfer chicken to cutting board, let cool slightly, then shred into bite-size pieces using 2 forks.

3 Meanwhile, stir asparagus and tomatoes into pasta. Cook, using highest sauté function, until pasta and asparagus are tender and sauce is thickened, 5 to 8 minutes. Stir in chicken and any accumulated juices, Parmesan, and basil. Season with salt and pepper to taste. Serve, passing extra Parmesan and basil separately.

photo on following page >

Parmesan Penne with
Chicken and Asparagus,
page 170

FUSILLI WITH Braised Pork, Fennel, and Lemon

2 tablespoons extra-virgin olive oil

1 large onion, chopped fine

6 garlic cloves, minced

1 tablespoon minced fresh thyme or 1 teaspoon dried

2 teaspoons fennel seeds

3 cups water

2 cups chicken broth

1 pound boneless country-style pork ribs, trimmed and cut into 1½-inch pieces

1 teaspoon table salt

1 teaspoon pepper

1 pound 100 percent whole-wheat fusilli

2 fennel bulbs, 2 tablespoons fronds minced, stalks discarded, bulbs halved, cored, and sliced thin, divided

2 ounces Pecorino Romano cheese, grated (1 cup), plus extra for serving

1½ teaspoons grated lemon zest plus ¼ cup juice (2 lemons)

WHY THIS RECIPE WORKS Braised pasta and meat dishes are often decadent and tomatoey. For a lighter approach, we focused on fennel and lemony goodness. Though pork butt is more traditional for braising, we opted for leaner boneless country-style pork ribs, which simply fell apart after cooking under pressure for 25 minutes. For this fennel-forward meal, we started by using fennel seeds as an aromatic, along with garlic and thyme. After the pork had finished cooking, we removed it and added some thinly sliced raw fennel to the pork cooking liquid with the pasta. After going under pressure, we stirred the shredded pork back into the pasta along with some Pecorino cheese and the remaining sliced fennel so they could wilt but still retain crunch. Last, we took the fronds (which often get thrown out) and sprinkled them on top as an herby garnish. Pecorino added a tangy, salty bite while transforming the sauce into something creamy and luscious. A drizzle of lemon juice woke up this fresh and satisfying meal. If using traditional pasta, decrease water to 2 cups. Do not substitute other pasta shapes in this recipe.

1 Using highest sauté function, heat oil in Instant Pot until shimmering. Add onion and cook until softened, about 5 minutes. Add garlic, thyme, and fennel seeds and cook, stirring frequently, until fragrant, about 30 seconds. Stir in water and broth, scraping up any browned bits, then stir in pork, salt, and pepper. Lock lid into place and close pressure-release valve. Select high pressure-cook function and cook for 25 minutes.

2 Turn off Instant Pot and quick-release pressure. Carefully remove lid, allowing steam to escape away from you. Using slotted spoon, transfer pork to cutting board, let cool slightly, then shred into bite-size pieces using 2 forks; discard excess fat.

3 Meanwhile, stir pasta and half of sliced fennel into pot. Lock lid into place and close pressure-release valve. Select high pressure-cook function and cook for 4 minutes. Turn off Instant Pot and quick-release pressure. Carefully remove lid, allowing steam to escape away from you.

Serves 4 to 6
Calories 470
Total Time 1½ hours

4 Stir Pecorino, shredded pork and any accumulated juices, and remaining fennel slices into pasta. Partially cover pot and let sit until pasta is tender, pork and fennel are heated through, and sauce is thickened, 5 to 8 minutes. Stir in lemon zest and juice and season with salt and pepper to taste. Sprinkle with fennel fronds and serve, passing extra Pecorino separately.

SPAGHETTI WITH Mushrooms, Kale, and Fontina

1 pound 100 percent whole-wheat spaghetti

1 tablespoon extra-virgin olive oil

1 pound cremini mushrooms, trimmed and quartered

½ teaspoon table salt

6 garlic cloves, minced

½ teaspoon red pepper flakes

2 cups vegetable or chicken broth

2 cups water

1 (28-ounce) can petite diced tomatoes

12 ounces kale, stemmed and chopped

4 ounces fontina cheese, shredded (1 cup)

WHY THIS RECIPE WORKS There's something satisfying about taking a bite of creamy pasta knowing that there is no cream in sight. This dish is deceptively healthy and incredibly simple to throw together for a weeknight meal. After cooking a pound of mushrooms, we added garlic and pepper flakes, then deglazed with vegetable broth and water. We didn't want this to be "marinara-y," so we used just canned diced tomatoes for textural contrast. Before cooking, we jam-packed the pot with antioxidant-loaded kale, which cooked on top of the whole-wheat spaghetti. For a creamy finish, we sprinkled everything with fontina and let it sit for "the magical 5 minutes," at which time the now-thickened sauce and cheese came together to form a delicious and healthy meal.

---

1 Loosely wrap half of pasta in dish towel, then press bundle against corner of counter to break noodles into 6-inch lengths; repeat with remaining pasta. Set aside.

2 Using highest sauté function, heat oil in Instant Pot until shimmering. Add mushrooms and salt, partially cover pot, and cook, stirring occasionally, until mushrooms release their liquid, about 5 minutes. Uncover and continue to cook until liquid has mostly evaporated, 3 to 5 minutes.

3 Add garlic and pepper flakes and cook, stirring frequently, until fragrant, about 30 seconds. Stir in broth and water, scraping up any browned bits, then stir in tomatoes and their juice and spaghetti. Arrange kale in even layer on top of spaghetti.

4 Lock lid into place and close pressure-release valve. Select high pressure-cook function and cook for 6 minutes. Turn off Instant Pot and quick-release pressure. Carefully remove lid, allowing steam to escape away from you.

5 Stir fontina into pasta and kale. Partially cover pot and let sit until spaghetti is tender, kale is wilted, and sauce is thickened, 5 to 8 minutes. Season with salt and pepper to taste. Serve.

Serves 4 to 6
Calories 410
Total Time 1 hour

Serves 4 to 6
Calories 360
Total Time 45 minutes

CREAMY SPRING VEGETABLE LINGUINE

WHY THIS RECIPE WORKS This confoundingly uncomplicated pasta dish was a revelation to us: perfect al dente noodles in a silky sauce, with a vibrant mix of vegetables and flavors—but without multiple pots, boiling water, or messy draining. Linguine was our favored shape, as the thicker strands retained their bite in the ultrahigh heat of the Instant Pot. After cooking the pasta, we stirred in convenient jarred baby artichokes and frozen peas. By using exactly the right amount of water, we didn't need to drain the pasta; instead we captured all of the starch that the linguine released, which made it a cinch to emulsify grated Pecorino and the residual cooking liquid into a luscious sauce. To finish, lemon zest and fresh tarragon enlivened this springy, light dish. You can substitute traditional linguine for the whole-wheat linguine; however, do not substitute other pasta shapes. While we prefer the flavor and texture of jarred whole baby artichokes, you can substitute 6 ounces frozen artichoke halves, thawed and patted dry.

1 pound 100 percent whole-wheat linguine

5 cups water

1 tablespoon extra-virgin olive oil

1½ teaspoons table salt

1 cup jarred whole baby artichokes packed in water, quartered

1 cup frozen peas, thawed

4 ounces Pecorino Romano cheese, finely grated (2 cups), plus extra for serving

½ teaspoon pepper

2 teaspoons grated lemon zest

2 tablespoons chopped fresh tarragon

1 Loosely wrap half of pasta in dish towel, then press bundle against corner of counter to break noodles into 6-inch lengths; repeat with remaining pasta.

2 Add pasta, water, oil, and salt to Instant Pot, making sure pasta is completely submerged. Lock lid into place and close pressure-release valve. Select high pressure-cook function and cook for 4 minutes. Turn off Instant Pot and quick-release pressure. Carefully remove lid, allowing steam to escape away from you.

3 Stir artichokes and peas into pasta. Partially cover pot and let sit until pasta is tender, vegetables are heated through, and sauce is thickened, 5 to 8 minutes. Stir in Pecorino and pepper until cheese is melted and fully combined. Stir in lemon zest and tarragon and season with salt and pepper to taste. Serve, passing extra Pecorino separately.

RIGATONI WITH MUSHROOM RAGÙ

1½ pounds cremini mushrooms, trimmed and quartered

1 carrot, peeled and chopped

1 small onion, chopped

3 tablespoons extra-virgin olive oil

½ ounce dried porcini mushrooms, rinsed and minced

3 garlic cloves, minced

2 tablespoons tomato paste

¾ cup dry red wine

1 (28-ounce) can diced tomatoes

1 pound 100 percent whole-wheat rigatoni

2 cups vegetable or chicken broth

1½ cups water

1 tablespoon soy sauce

Grated Parmesan cheese

WHY THIS RECIPE WORKS With great success, mushrooms are frequently used as a meat alternative, so we set out to develop a mushroom version of a classic Italian-style meat sauce that would have long-cooked flavor and hearty texture. For complexity, we turned to two types of mushrooms: Dried porcini delivered depth of flavor, while a whopping 1½ pounds of fresh cremini gave the sauce substantial feel. To round out the sauce's umami qualities, we added a splash of soy sauce and some tomato paste, while a bit of red wine and diced tomatoes added the right amount of fruity acidity and body. To make prep easy, we used the food processor to chop the cremini, onion, and carrot. The key to success was pairing this rich sauce with the right pasta: Rigatoni proved to be a great match, with its sturdy body (to stand up to the heavy sauce) and its delicate ridges (to which the sauce could adhere). After cooking everything under pressure, we let the pasta and sauce rest until the sauce was perfectly thickened. A sprinkle of grated Parmesan cheese was a simple, classic finish. If using traditional pasta, decrease the water to ¾ cup. Do not substitute other pasta shapes in this recipe.

1 Working in batches, pulse cremini mushrooms in food processor until pieces are no larger than ½ inch, 5 to 7 pulses; transfer to large bowl. Pulse carrot and onion in now-empty processor until finely chopped, 5 to 7 pulses; transfer to bowl with mushrooms.

2 Using highest sauté function, heat oil in Instant Pot until shimmering. Add processed vegetables and porcini mushrooms, partially cover pot, and cook, stirring occasionally, until vegetables release their liquid, about 5 minutes. Uncover and continue to cook until liquid has evaporated and vegetables begin to brown, 8 to 10 minutes.

3 Add garlic and tomato paste and cook, stirring frequently, until fragrant, about 30 seconds. Stir in wine, scraping up any browned bits, and cook until mostly evaporated, about 1 minute. Stir in tomatoes and their juice, rigatoni, broth, water, and soy sauce.

4 Lock lid into place and close pressure-release valve. Select high pressure-cook function and cook for 5 minutes. Turn off Instant Pot and quick-release pressure. Carefully remove lid, allowing steam to escape away from you.

5 Stir rigatoni and sauce to combine. Partially cover pot and let sit until rigatoni is tender and sauce is thickened, 5 to 8 minutes. Season with salt and pepper to taste. Serve, passing Parmesan separately.

SHELLS WITH Butternut Squash, Leeks, and Burrata

2 tablespoons extra-virgin olive oil

1 pound leeks, halved lengthwise, sliced 1 inch thick, and washed thoroughly

4 garlic cloves, minced

½ teaspoon red pepper flakes

3 cups vegetable or chicken broth

2 cups water

1 pound 100 percent whole-wheat medium pasta shells

1½ pounds butternut squash, peeled, seeded, and cut into ½-inch pieces (5 cups)

¾ teaspoon table salt

2 teaspoons grated lemon zest, divided, plus 1 tablespoon juice

2 tablespoons minced fresh tarragon, divided

8 ounces burrata cheese, room temperature

¼ cup toasted chopped walnuts

WHY THIS RECIPE WORKS Butternut squash and pasta have gotten along for years (ravioli, anyone?), so we thought we'd deconstruct the often butter-coated duo in a healthier way, without skimping on the decadence. We started with an aromatic base full of pepper flakes, garlic, and lots of leeks (even the often-thrown-away-yet-nutrient-rich green parts), then pressure-cooked our pasta with lots of little gem-size pieces of butternut squash. To balance the rich aspect of this sauce, we contrasted with a healthy amount of lemon zest and fresh tarragon. The savory, subtle anise flavor of tarragon was a surprise alternative to the more common match of butternut squash and sage. Arranging creamy burrata on top turned this dish into a more sophisticated and luxurious meal. If using traditional pasta, decrease the water to 1 cup. Do not substitute other pasta shapes in this recipe. If burrata is unavailable, substitute fresh mozzarella.

1 Using highest sauté function, heat oil in Instant Pot until shimmering. Add leeks and cook until softened and lightly browned, 3 to 5 minutes. Add garlic and pepper flakes and cook, stirring frequently, until fragrant, about 30 seconds. Stir in broth and water, scraping up any browned bits, then stir in pasta, squash, and salt.

2 Lock lid into place and close pressure-release valve. Select high pressure-cook function and cook for 6 minutes. Turn off Instant Pot and quick-release pressure. Carefully remove lid, allowing steam to escape away from you.

3 Stir shells and sauce to combine. Partially cover pot and let sit until shells are tender and sauce is thickened, 5 to 8 minutes. Stir in 1 teaspoon lemon zest and juice and 1 tablespoon tarragon. Season with salt and pepper to taste. Transfer pasta to serving platter.

4 Cut burrata into rough 1½-inch pieces, collecting creamy liquid. Arrange burrata on top of pasta and drizzle with creamy liquid. Sprinkle with walnuts, remaining 1 teaspoon lemon zest, and remaining 1 tablespoon tarragon. Serve.

Serves 4 to 6
Calories 510
Total Time 1 hour

FIDEOS

WITH Chickpeas, Fennel, and Spinach

8 ounces 100 percent whole-wheat spaghetti

2 tablespoons extra-virgin olive oil

1 onion, chopped fine

1 fennel bulb, 1 tablespoon fronds minced, stalks discarded, bulb halved, cored, and sliced thin

3 garlic cloves, minced

1½ teaspoons smoked paprika

1½ cups vegetable or chicken broth

1 (15-ounce) can chickpeas, rinsed

1 (14.5-ounce) can diced tomatoes

¼ cup dry white wine

¼ teaspoon table salt

¼ teaspoon pepper

4 ounces (4 cups) baby spinach

¼ cup sliced almonds, toasted

Lemon wedges

WHY THIS RECIPE WORKS Fideos, traditional to Spanish cooking, is a richly flavored dish in which thin noodles are toasted until nut-brown, then cooked in a garlicky, tomatoey sauce, sometimes with seafood. Recipes often include a homemade stock, a sofrito base of slowly reduced fresh tomatoes with seasonings, and time in the oven. The complex flavors are undeniably exciting, but the preparation can be time-consuming. For a one-pot version that cut down on time, whole-wheat pasta, which is inherently nutty, was a convenient shortcut. We streamlined the sofrito base by finely chopping onion (so it softened and browned quickly with the sauté function), thinly slicing fennel, and using canned tomatoes instead of fresh. Garlic, smoked paprika, and wine added even more depth to the broth. For our vegetarian version, we chose hearty, creamy canned chickpeas. After cooking everything under pressure, we stirred spinach into the pasta to wilt while the sauce thickened. A final garnish of fennel fronds and almonds provided a welcome textural contrast. You can substitute traditional spaghetti for the whole-wheat spaghetti; however, do not substitute other pasta shapes. If your fennel bulb does not come with fronds, substitute 1 tablespoon chopped fresh dill or parsley for the fronds.

1   Loosely wrap pasta in dish towel, then press bundle against corner of counter to break noodles into 1- to 2-inch lengths.

2   Using highest sauté function, heat oil in Instant Pot until shimmering. Add onion and sliced fennel and cook until softened, about 5 minutes. Add spaghetti and cook, stirring frequently, until lightly toasted, about 2 minutes.

3   Add garlic and paprika and cook, stirring frequently, until fragrant, about 30 seconds. Stir in broth, chickpeas, tomatoes and their juice, wine, salt, and pepper.

Serves 4
Calories 420
Total Time 45 minutes

4 Lock lid into place and close pressure-release valve. Select high pressure-cook function and cook for 1 minute. Turn off Instant Pot and quick-release pressure. Carefully remove lid, allowing steam to escape away from you.

5 Stir spinach into pasta. Partially cover pot and let sit until pasta is tender and sauce is thickened, 5 to 8 minutes. Season with salt and pepper to taste. Sprinkle with fennel fronds and almonds, and serve with lemon wedges.

SOPA SECA WITH Chorizo and Black Beans

8 ounces 100 percent whole-wheat spaghetti

1 tablespoon extra-virgin olive oil

1 onion, chopped

1 green bell pepper, stemmed, seeded, and chopped

4 ounces Mexican-style chorizo sausage, casings removed

2 tablespoons minced canned chipotle chile in adobo sauce

2 tablespoons tomato paste

3 garlic cloves, minced

1 cup chicken broth

1 cup water

1 (15-ounce) can black beans, rinsed

10 ounces cherry tomatoes, halved

1 avocado, halved, pitted, and cut into 1-inch pieces

1 ounce cotija cheese, crumbled (¼ cup)

½ cup fresh cilantro leaves

Lime wedges

WHY THIS RECIPE WORKS Traditional versions of this vibrant one-pot pasta dish—in which thin strands of fideos pasta are toasted until golden and then cooked in a tasty broth until the broth has reduced to a thick sauce—are a popular Mexican specialty. We started by creating a robust sofrito of onion, bell pepper, and Mexican chorizo. Thanks to the intense heat of the sauté function, we were able to lightly toast the pasta in this flavorful mixture before stirring in chipotle chile in adobo sauce, tomato paste, and minced garlic. Next, we stirred in a measured amount of chicken broth along with black beans for added protein. In just 1 minute under pressure, the pasta was al dente and the liquid nearly absorbed. We gave the still-hot pot a quick stir (and also threw in halved cherry tomatoes) and a brief rest to enable the pasta to finish cooking gently and the sauce to thicken. To complement the deep, earthy, spicy flavors of the pasta, we finished with an array of fresh, tangy garnishes—chopped avocado, crumbled cotija cheese, fresh cilantro, and lime wedges. You can substitute traditional spaghetti for the whole-wheat spaghetti; however, do not substitute other pasta shapes. Be sure to use fresh Mexican chorizo here, not the semicured Spanish or Portuguese versions.

1   Loosely wrap half of pasta in dish towel, then press bundle against corner of counter to break noodles into 1- to 2-inch lengths; repeat with remaining pasta. Set aside.

2   Using highest sauté function, heat oil in Instant Pot until shimmering. Add onion, bell pepper, and chorizo and cook, breaking up meat with wooden spoon, until vegetables are softened, 3 to 5 minutes.

3   Add spaghetti and cook, stirring frequently, until lightly toasted, about 2 minutes. Add chipotle, tomato paste, and garlic and cook, stirring frequently, until fragrant, about 30 seconds. Stir in broth and water, scraping up any browned bits, then stir in beans.

Serves 4
Calories 550
Total Time 50 minutes

4   Lock lid into place and close pressure-release valve. Select high pressure-cook function and cook for 1 minute. Turn off Instant Pot and quick-release pressure. Carefully remove lid, allowing steam to escape away from you.

5   Stir tomatoes into pasta mixture. Partially cover pot and let sit until pasta is tender and sauce is thickened, 5 to 8 minutes. Season with salt and pepper to taste. Sprinkle individual portions with avocado, cotija, and cilantro. Serve with lime wedges.

SWEET AND SAVORY RICE NOODLES
WITH Chicken and Green Beans

⅓ cup unseasoned rice vinegar

1 serrano chile, stemmed and sliced into thin rings

5 teaspoons canola oil, divided

3 garlic cloves, sliced thin

3 tablespoons oyster sauce

2 tablespoons packed dark brown sugar

1 tablespoon fish sauce, plus extra for seasoning

1½ pounds boneless, skinless chicken thighs, trimmed and quartered

8 ounces (¼-inch-wide) rice noodles

12 ounces green beans, trimmed and halved crosswise

½ cup chopped fresh cilantro

½ cup dry-roasted peanuts, chopped coarse

WHY THIS RECIPE WORKS There's nothing like a warm, umami-forward bowl of soupy rice noodles, especially when it's topped with a quick-pickled spicy serrano. We opted for boneless, skinless chicken thighs, which we pressure-cooked in a savory (very pantry-friendly) sauce of oyster sauce, brown sugar, and fish sauce. Not only did this mixture impart a great deal of flavor into the chicken, it also transformed itself into the broth-y component to this noodle dish. We tossed a healthy portion of vitamin-rich green beans into the broth to cook while staying bright green and crisp-tender. Topping the noodles with fresh cilantro and crunchy peanuts offered a refreshing complement to the dish. Don't forget to drizzle with vinegar for a zingy topping. To make this dish spicier, reserve and add the serrano seeds.

1   Combine vinegar and serrano in bowl. Let sit at room temperature for at least 15 minutes. (Chile vinegar can be efrigerated for up to 3 days.)

2   Using highest sauté function, cook 3 teaspoons oil and garlic in Instant Pot until fragrant, about 3 minutes. Stir in 2 cups water, oyster sauce, sugar, and fish sauce, scraping up any browned bits, then stir in chicken.

3   Lock lid into place and close pressure-release valve. Select high pressure-cook function and cook for 9 minutes. Turn off Instant Pot and quick-release pressure. Carefully remove lid, allowing steam to escape away from you.

4   Meanwhile, place noodles in large bowl, cover with boiling water, and let soak until almost tender, about 8 minutes, stirring occasionally. Drain noodles and rinse under cold running water until chilled. Drain noodles well again and toss with remaining 2 teaspoons oil; set aside.

Serves 4 to 6
Calories 430
Total Time 1 hour

5   Using slotted spoon, transfer chicken to cutting board. Let chicken cool slightly, then shred into bite-size pieces using 2 forks. Add green beans to broth remaining in pot. Partially cover and cook, using lowest sauté function, until green beans are crisp-tender, 3 to 5 minutes.

6   Turn off Instant Pot. Stir in noodles and chicken and any accumulated juices and cook, using residual heat, until noodles are tender and chicken is warmed through, about 3 minutes. Season with extra fish sauce to taste. Sprinkle individual portions with cilantro and peanuts. Serve, passing chile vinegar separately.

Serves 4 to 6
Calories 460
Total Time 1¼ hours

GINGER RAMEN NOODLES
WITH Beef and Bok Choy

WHY THIS RECIPE WORKS Instant ramen may come with microwave instructions, but breakroom preparation doesn't do them justice. Instead of using the salty flavor packet with vague ingredients, we built our own healthier sauce. A mix of ginger, garlic, sake, and soy sauce was easy but elegant enough to combine with meltingly tender boneless beef short ribs that needed only 25 minutes to cook (with some shiitakes). We then nestled the uncooked noodles into the braising liquid and simmered them until they were chewy. Baby bok choy, quick cooking and crunchy, was a welcome vegetable to round out the noodles and beef. A sprinkle of shichimi togarashi (a seven-spice mix with toasted sesame seeds, dried chiles, and nori flakes) provided a salty, spicy kick. You can substitute boneless beef chuck-eye roast for the short ribs. If using larger bok choy, halve them, then cut into 2-inch pieces.

1. Using highest sauté function, heat oil in Instant Pot until shimmering. Add garlic and ginger and cook, stirring frequently, until fragrant, about 30 seconds. Stir in broth, water, sake, and soy sauce, then stir in beef and mushrooms. Lock lid into place and close pressure-release valve. Select high pressure-cook function and cook for 25 minutes.

2. Turn off Instant Pot and quick-release pressure. Carefully remove lid, allowing steam to escape away from you. Nestle noodles in even layer into pot (you may need to break noodles to fit). Partially cover pot and cook, using highest sauté function, until noodles have softened on bottom, about 3 minutes. Uncover pot, flip noodles, and stir to separate.

3. Stir in bok choy and cook, tossing occasionally, until noodles and bok choy are tender and broth has thickened slightly, about 2 minutes. Season with extra soy sauce to taste. Divide noodles evenly among serving bowls and sprinkle with scallions. Serve, passing shichimi togarashi separately.

1 tablespoon canola oil

3 garlic cloves, minced

1 tablespoon grated fresh ginger

1½ cups chicken or vegetable broth

1½ cups water

¼ cup sake or dry white wine

1½ tablespoons soy sauce, plus extra for seasoning

1 pound boneless beef short ribs, trimmed and cut into 1-inch pieces

8 ounces shiitake mushrooms, stemmed and sliced thin

4 (3-ounce) packages ramen noodles, seasoning packets discarded

6 small heads baby bok choy (about 3 ounces each), trimmed and halved lengthwise

4 scallions, sliced thin on bias

Shichimi togarashi

SWEET POTATO GLASS NOODLES
WITH Portobellos and Spinach

2 tablespoons canola oil

1 onion, halved and sliced thin

1-2 tablespoons gochujang paste

3 garlic cloves, minced

1 tablespoon grated fresh ginger

½ cup vegetable or chicken broth

2 tablespoons soy sauce, plus extra for seasoning

1 pound portobello mushroom caps, gills removed, sliced ½ inch thick

8 ounces (⅛-inch-wide) dried sweet potato glass noodles, broken into 12-inch lengths

2 teaspoons toasted sesame oil, plus extra for serving

8 ounces (8 cups) baby spinach

2 carrots, peeled and cut into 2-inch-long matchsticks

6 scallions, sliced thin on bias, divided

1 tablespoon sesame seeds, toasted

WHY THIS RECIPE WORKS This dish takes its cue from a popular Korean dish known as japchae, which combines sweet potato starch noodles with a variety of colorful vegetables (and sometimes meat) in a savory, sesame-forward sauce with a touch of sweetness. This appealing profile was the starting point for our meatless noodle dish that took advantage of the Instant Pot's cook functions to create a hearty combination of flavors and textures that echoed our favorite qualities of japchae. In lieu of the beef and shiitake mushrooms often found in japchae, we turned to meaty and hefty portobello mushrooms, which, when cut into strips and cooked under pressure, emerged as the stars of this dish. To unite the elements, we simply stirred our partially rehydrated noodles, scallions, carrots, and a hearty pile of baby spinach into the pot already containing cooked onion, gochujang, garlic, ginger, soy sauce, and a splash of broth. Tossing everything over gentle heat turned the vegetables tender and the sauce perfectly thickened. A sprinkle of toasted sesame seeds and fresh scallions made for a well-rounded finish. If you can't find sweet potato glass noodles (also known as sweet potato starch noodles), substitute bean thread (cellophane) noodles. For a milder dish, use the lesser amount of gochujang.

1 Using highest sauté function, heat canola oil in Instant Pot until shimmering. Add onion and cook until softened and lightly browned, 3 to 5 minutes. Add gochujang paste, garlic, and ginger and cook, stirring frequently, until fragrant, about 30 seconds. Stir in broth and soy sauce, scraping up any browned bits, then stir in mushrooms.

2 Lock lid into place and close pressure-release valve. Select high pressure-cook function and cook for 5 minutes. Turn off Instant Pot and quick-release pressure. Carefully remove lid, allowing steam to escape away from you.

Serves 4
Calories 260
Total Time 45 minutes

3 Meanwhile, place noodles in large bowl, cover with boiling water, and let soak until almost tender, about 8 minutes, stirring occasionally. Drain noodles and rinse under cold running water until chilled. Drain noodles well again and toss with sesame oil.

4 Stir noodles, spinach, carrots, and two-thirds of scallions into mushroom mixture. Using highest sauté function, cook, tossing gently with tongs, until noodles and vegetables are tender and sauce is slightly thickened, about 3 minutes. Season with soy sauce to taste. Sprinkle individual portions with remaining scallions and sesame seeds. Serve, passing extra sesame oil separately.

NUTRITIONAL INFORMATION FOR OUR RECIPES

To calculate the nutritional values of our recipes per serving, we used The Food Processor SQL by ESHA Research. We entered all the ingredients for each recipe, using weights for important ingredients such as most vegetables. We also used our preferred brands in these analyses. We did not include additional salt or pepper for food that's "seasoned to taste." For recipes with a range in the number of servings, we used the highest number in the range to calculate the nutritional values.

	Calories	Total Fat (G)	Sat Fat (G)	Chol (MG)	Sodium (MG)	Total Carbs (G)	Fiber (G)	Total Sugar (G)	Added Sugar (G)	Protein (G)
CHICKEN										
Chicken Noodle Soup with Shells, Tomatoes, and Zucchini	480	12	2.5	210	1000	21	3	6	0	69
Chicken Harira	340	14	2	65	1100	24	6	4	0	30
White Chicken Chili with Zucchini	340	8	1	90	880	29	15	4	0	33
Smoky Turkey Meatball Soup with Kale and Manchego	310	12	4.5	50	1030	14	3	5	0	38
Chicken with Warm Bread and Arugula Salad	530	31	6	85	810	28	3	8	0	33
Chicken and Braised Radishes with Dukkah	410	20	3.5	130	760	14	4	5	0	45
Chicken and Barley Risotto with Butternut Squash and Kale	570	21	7	100	780	51	11	5	0	39
Chipotle Chicken and Black Beans with Pickled Cabbage	440	24	6	120	770	32	1	4	1	29
Javaher Polo with Chicken	760	29	5	90	890	87	4	29	0	39
Chicken with Spring Vegetables	470	24	6	120	840	34	7	8	0	30
Chicken with Spiced Whole Parsnips and Scallion-Mint Relish	620	39	8	120	810	43	11	14	4	25
Chicken and Potatoes with Fennel and Saffron	480	28	6	120	760	26	1	5	0	24
Soy Sauce Chicken with Gai Lan	380	25	6	120	800	14	5	5	3	24
Chicken and Couscous with Prunes and Olives	520	27	6	120	810	62	9	18	0	28
Chicken and Black Rice Bowl with Peanut-Sesame Dressing	600	20	3	135	800	63	8	6	1	47

	Calories	Total Fat (G)	Sat Fat (G)	Chol (MG)	Sodium (MG)	Total Carbs (G)	Fiber (G)	Total Sugar (G)	Added Sugar (G)	Protein (G)
CHICKEN (CONT.)										
Shredded Chicken Tacos with Mango Salsa	560	18	4	150	710	60	3	19	0	44
Chicken Sausages with White Beans and Spinach	410	23	4.5	180	1040	22	5	3	0	25
Chicken in a Pot with Mashed Root Vegetables	530	33	9	150	760	19	4	6	0	39
BEEF, PORK, AND LAMB										
Double Vegetable Beef Stew with Lemon Zest	360	11	3	75	800	30	5	8	0	31
Hawaiian Oxtail Soup	520	29	10	170	1090	13	4	4	0	52
Seared Flank Steak with White Bean and Sun-Dried Tomato Salad	490	25	6	75	990	32	8	1	0	35
Steak Tips with Warm Potato and Green Bean Salad	430	20	5	80	730	33	5	6	0	29
Braised Short Ribs with Daikon and Shiitakes	500	16	5	65	800	47	6	20	6	27
Boneless Short Ribs and Cauliflower Puttanesca	340	17	6	70	980	19	6	9	0	28
Shredded Beef Tacos with Jicama Slaw	400	13	3	75	500	40	5	7	1	30
Caldo Verde	500	31	9	50	1060	33	2	2	0	22
Pork Pozole Rojo	400	17	3	85	920	35	1	2	0	27
Smothered Pork Chops with Leeks and Mustard	550	17	5	95	780	13	1	3	0	35
Pork and Bulgur Bowls with Parsley-Pepita Sauce	550	25	5	85	750	50	9	6	3	33
Creamy Parmesan Polenta with Eggplant, Sausage, and Tomatoes	420	22	7	45	1060	30	5	4	0	28
Abgoosht	570	9	2.5	65	980	89	2	6	0	41
Lamb Meatballs with Creamy Lemon and Feta Orzo	670	31	13	90	940	65	12	6	0	35
SEAFOOD										
New England Fish Chowder	480	11	2	5	660	39	1	4	0	12
Swordfish Stew with Tomatoes, Capers, and Pine Nuts	320	19	4	20	210	1	0	1	0	1
Calamari, Chorizo, and Chickpea Stew	390	13	2.5	10	380	3	1	1	0	2

	Calories	Total Fat (G)	Sat Fat (G)	Chol (MG)	Sodium (MG)	Total Carbs (G)	Fiber (G)	Total Sugar (G)	Added Sugar (G)	Protein (G)
SEAFOOD (CONT.)										
Salmon Niçoise Salad	580	0	0	0	2580	38	11	17	0	6
Salmon with Spiced Chickpea, Cucumber, and Tomato Salad	540	14	2	0	330	10	3	0	0	5
Salmon with Wild Rice and Orange Salad	680	28	4	5	360	3	1	0	1	4
Salmon with Ponzu-Braised Eggplant	490	11	1.5	0	1070	13	2	8	4	2
Haddock with Tomatoes, Escarole, and Crispy Garlic	310	0	0	0	40	15	2	13	0	0
Swordfish with Braised Green Beans, Tomatoes, and Feta	470	17	4.5	120	740	38	3	9	0	41
Halibut with Lentils, Kale, and Pancetta	480	4.5	0.5	0	75	7	2	2	0	8
Halibut with Couscous and Ras el Hanout	540	1	0	0	75	18	0	0	0	2
Southwestern Shrimp and Oat Berry Bowl	610	18	1.5	0	75	8	4	2	0	7
Shrimp and White Beans with Butternut Squash and Sage	370	1.5	0	0	75	13	2	0	0	2
Shrimp Jambalaya	350	1.5	1	5	95	20	4	13	0	3
Mussels with Red Curry and Coconut Rice	420	6	1	0	95	21	4	8	2	3
VEGETABLES AND GRAINS										
Hearty Minestrone	270	10	1.5	0	850	34	17	7	0	11
Green Gumbo	380	20	1.5	0	890	42	12	8	0	13
Spiced Wild Rice and Coconut Soup	360	25	19	0	820	30	3	3	0	8
Bean and Sweet Potato Chili	400	8	1	0	810	67	6	13	0	16
Green Shakshuka	310	19	4.5	190	830	22	8	6	0	16
Baba Ghanoush with Chickpea and Arugula Salad	570	29	4.5	185	790	61	11	15	4	21
Sherry-Braised Leeks on Toast with Red Pepper–Hazelnut Relish	370	24	6	10	740	28	3	7	0	10
Braised Cabbage Wedges with Curry Powder and Chickpeas	400	21	2	5	870	42	13	12	0	13
Black Beans and Brown Rice	330	5	0	0	820	65	5	6	0	12
Chana Masala	270	13	1	0	930	45	3	5	0	12

	Calories	Total Fat (G)	Sat Fat (G)	Chol (MG)	Sodium (MG)	Total Carbs (G)	Fiber (G)	Total Sugar (G)	Added Sugar (G)	Protein (G)
VEGETABLES AND GRAINS (CONT.)										
Braised Lentils and Tofu with Thai Green Curry	310	11	6	0	890	30	5	6	0	21
Braised Tofu with Pumpkin Mole and Apple-Cabbage Slaw	320	10	3.5	15	840	43	2	28	1	16
Gochujang-Braised Tempeh Lettuce Wraps	380	19	4.5	0	530	30	3	14	9	29
Farro Salad with Asparagus, Snap Peas, and Tomatoes	290	11	2.5	10	350	42	6	5	0	9
Smoky Paprika Rice with Crispy Artichokes and Peppers	410	11	1.5	0	880	69	7	7	0	9
Savory Oatmeal with Sautéed Wild Mushrooms	560	26	6	20	840	64	11	4	0	16
PASTA AND NOODLES										
Spaghetti and Turkey Meatballs	460	10	3	65	900	61	11	8	0	34
Parmesan Penne with Chicken and Asparagus	440	11	2.5	50	870	53	10	4	0	28
Fusilli with Braised Pork, Fennel, and Lemon	470	14	3.5	65	800	57	11	6	0	30
Spaghetti with Mushrooms, Kale, and Fontina	410	11	4	20	880	61	12	8	0	19
Creamy Spring Vegetable Linguine	360	9	3.5	20	870	51	9	3	0	17
Rigatoni with Mushroom Ragù	410	10	1	0	840	63	9	10	0	14
Shells with Butternut Squash, Leeks, and Burrata	510	20	6	25	810	71	12	7	0	20
Fideos with Chickpeas, Fennel, and Spinach	420	13	1.5	0	850	61	15	8	0	15
Sopa Seca with Chorizo and Black Beans	550	26	7	30	890	63	12	7	0	22
Sweet and Savory Rice Noodles with Chicken and Green Beans	430	15	2.5	105	580	44	3	7	4	30
Ginger Ramen Noodles with Beef and Bok Choy	460	21	6	45	950	45	4	2	0	24
Sweet Potato Glass Noodles with Portobellos and Spinach	260	11	1	0	710	36	5	11	0	7

CONVERSIONS AND EQUIVALENTS

Some say cooking is a science and an art. We would say that geography has a hand in it, too. Flours and sugars manufactured in the United Kingdom and elsewhere will feel and taste different from those manufactured in the United States. So we cannot promise that the loaf of bread you bake in Canada or England will taste the same as a loaf baked in the States, but we can offer guidelines for converting weights and measures. We also recommend that you rely on your instincts when making our recipes. Refer to the visual cues provided. If the dough hasn't "come together in a ball" as described, you may need to add more flour—even if the recipe doesn't tell you to. You be the judge.

The recipes in this book were developed using standard U.S. measures following U.S. government guidelines. The charts below offer equivalents for U.S. and metric measures. All conversions are approximate and have been rounded up or down to the nearest whole number.

EXAMPLE

1 teaspoon = 4.9292 milliliters, rounded up to 5 milliliters

1 ounce = 28.3495 grams, rounded down to 28 grams

VOLUME CONVERSIONS

U.S.	METRIC
1 teaspoon	5 milliliters
2 teaspoons	10 milliliters
1 tablespoon	15 milliliters
2 tablespoons	30 milliliters
¼ cup	59 milliliters
⅓ cup	79 milliliters
½ cup	118 milliliters
¾ cup	177 milliliters
1 cup	237 milliliters
1¼ cups	296 milliliters
1½ cups	355 milliliters
2 cups (1 pint)	473 milliliters
2½ cups	591 milliliters
3 cups	710 milliliters
4 cups (1 quart)	0.946 liter
1.06 quarts	1 liter
4 quarts (1 gallon)	3.8 liters

WEIGHT CONVERSIONS

OUNCES	GRAMS
½	14
¾	21
1	28
1½	43
2	57
2½	71
3	85
3½	99
4	113
4½	128
5	142
6	170
7	198
8	227
9	255
10	283
12	340
16 (1 pound)	454

INDEX

Note: Page references in *italics* indicate recipe photographs.

A

Abgoosht, 90-91, *92-93*
Apple Cider-Sage Vinaigrette, 14
Artichokes and Peppers, Crispy,
    Smoky Paprika Rice with,
    162-63, *163*
Arugula
    and Bread Salad, Warm, Chicken
        with, 30-31, *32-33*
    and Chickpea Salad, Baba
        Ghanoush with, 142-43,
        144-45
Asparagus
    and Chicken, Parmesan Penne
        with, 170-71, *172-73*
    Snap Peas, and Tomatoes, Farro
        Salad with, 160, *161*

B

Baba Ghanoush with Chickpea
    and Arugula Salad, 142-43,
    144-45
Barley Risotto and Chicken with
    Butternut Squash and Kale,
    36-37, *37*
Basil Pesto, Classic, 16, *16*
Bean(s)
    Black, and Brown Rice, *150*, 151
    Black, and Chipotle Chicken with
        Pickled Cabbage, 38-39, *39*
    Black, and Chorizo, Sopa Seca
        with, 186-87, *187*
    cooking instructions, 10

Bean(s) (*cont.*)
    cook times, 10
    Green Gumbo, 134, *135*
    Hearty Minestrone, *132*, 133
    and Sweet Potato Chili, 138, *139*
    White, and Shrimp with
        Butternut Squash and Sage,
        124, 125
    White, and Spinach, Chicken
        Sausages with, *58*, 59
    White, and Sun-Dried Tomato
        Salad, Seared Flank Steak
        with, 70-71, *71*
    White Chicken Chili with
        Zucchini, 26-27, *27*
    see also Chickpea(s);
        Green Bean(s)
Beef
    and Bok Choy, Ginger Ramen
        Noodles with, *190*, 191
    Boneless Short Ribs and
        Cauliflower Puttanesca,
        76-77, *77*
    Braised Short Ribs with Daikon
        and Shiitakes, 74-75, *75*
    Hawaiian Oxtail Soup, 66-67,
        68-69
    Seared Flank Steak with White
        Bean and Sun-Dried Tomato
        Salad, 70-71, *71*
    Shredded, Tacos with Jicama
        Slaw, 78-79, *79*
    Steak Tips with Warm Potato and
        Green Bean Salad, 72-73, *73*
    Stew, Double Vegetable, with
        Lemon Zest, 64-65, *65*
Bok Choy and Beef, Ginger Ramen
    Noodles with, *190*, 191

Bread and Arugula Salad, Warm,
    Chicken with, 30-31, *32-33*
Bulgur and Pork Bowls with
    Parsley-Pepita Sauce, 86-87, *87*

C

Cabbage
    -Apple Slaw and Pumpkin Mole,
        Braised Tofu with, 156-57, *157*
    Hearty Minestrone, *132*, 133
    Pickled, Chipotle Chicken and
        Black Beans with, 38-39, *39*
    Wedges, Braised, with Curry
        Powder and Chickpeas,
        148-49, *149*
Calamari, Chorizo, and Chickpea
    Stew, 102, *103*
Caldo Verde, 80, *81*
Cashews
    Creamless Creamy Dressing, 17
Cauliflower Puttanesca and
    Boneless Short Ribs, 76-77, *77*
Chana Masala, 152-53, *153*
Cheese
    Creamy Parmesan Polenta
        with Eggplant, Sausage, and
        Tomatoes, 88-89, *89*
    Creamy Spring Vegetable
        Linguine, *178*, 179
    Lamb Meatballs with Creamy
        Lemon and Feta Orzo,
        94-95, *95*
    Parmesan Penne with Chicken
        and Asparagus, 170-71, *172-73*

Cheese (*cont.*)

Shells with Butternut Squash, Leeks, and Burrata, 182-83, *183*

Smoky Turkey Meatball Soup with Kale and Manchego, 28, *29*

Spaghetti with Mushrooms, Kale, and Fontina, 176, *177*

Chicken

and Asparagus, Parmesan Penne with, 170-71, *172-73*

and Barley Risotto with Butternut Squash and Kale, 36-37, *37*

and Black Rice Bowl with Peanut-Sesame Dressing, 54, *55*

and Braised Radishes with Dukkah, 34-35, *35*

Chili, White, with Zucchini, 26-27, *27*

Chipotle, and Black Beans with Pickled Cabbage, 38-39, *39*

and Couscous with Prunes and Olives, 52-53, *53*

and Green Beans, Sweet and Savory Rice Noodles with, 188-89, *189*

Harira, 24, *25*

Javaher Polo with, 40-41, *42-43*

Noodle Soup with Shells, Tomatoes, and Zucchini, *22*, 23

and Potatoes with Fennel and Saffron, *48*, 49

in a Pot with Mashed Root Vegetables, 60-61, *61*

Shredded, Tacos with Mango Salsa, *56*, 57

Soy Sauce, with Gai Lan, 50-51, *51*

with Spiced Whole Parsnips and Scallion-Mint Relish, 46-47, *47*

with Spring Vegetables, 44-45, *45*

with Warm Bread and Arugula Salad, 30-31, *32-33*

Chicken Sausages with White Beans and Spinach, *58*, 59

Chickpea(s)

Abgoosht, 90-91, *92-93*

and Arugula Salad, Baba Ghanoush with, 142-43, *144-45*

Calamari, and Chorizo Stew, 102, *103*

Chana Masala, 152-53, *153*

Cucumber, and Tomato Salad, Spiced, Salmon with, 108, *109*

and Curry Powder, Braised Cabbage Wedges with, 148-49, *149*

Fennel, and Spinach, Fideos with, 184-85, *185*

Chiles

Chana Masala, 152-53, *153*

Chipotle Chicken and Black Beans with Pickled Cabbage, 38-39, *39*

Chipotle-Yogurt Sauce, 17

Zhoug, 143, *145*

Chili

Bean and Sweet Potato, 138, *139*

White Chicken, with Zucchini, 26-27, *27*

Chowder, New England Fish, 98-99, *99*

Cilantro

Herb-Yogurt Sauce, 17, *17*

Zhoug, 143, *145*

Coconut

Rice and Red Curry, Mussels with, 128-29, *129*

and Wild Rice Soup, Spiced, *136*, 137

Collard greens

Caldo Verde, *80*, 81

Green Gumbo, 134, *135*

Couscous

and Chicken with Prunes and Olives, 52-53, *53*

Couscous (*cont.*)

and Ras el Hanout, Halibut with, 120-21, *121*

Cucumber, Chickpea, and Tomato Salad, Spiced, Salmon with, 108, *109*

Curry

Red, and Coconut Rice, Mussels with, 128-29, *129*

Thai Green, Braised Lentils and Tofu with, *154*, 155

D

Daikon and Shiitakes, Braised Short Ribs with, 74-75, *75*

Dressings

Apple Cider-Sage Vinaigrette, 14

Creamless Creamy, 17

Orange-Ginger Vinaigrette, 14

Pomegranate-Honey Vinaigrette, 14, *14*

Sriracha-Lime Vinaigrette, 15, *15*

E

Eggplant

Baba Ghanoush with Chickpea and Arugula Salad, 142-43, *144-45*

Ponzu-Braised, Salmon with, *112*, 113

Sausage, and Tomatoes, Creamy Parmesan Polenta with, 88-89, *89*

Eggs

Baba Ghanoush with Chickpea and Arugula Salad, 142-43, *144-45*

Eggs (*cont.*)

Green Shakshuka, 140-41, *141*

Hard- or Soft-Cooked, 19

Salmon Niçoise Salad, 104-5, *106-7*

Escarole, Tomatoes, and Crispy Garlic, Haddock with, 114-15, *115*

Everything Bagel Blend, 18

F

Farro Salad with Asparagus, Snap Peas, and Tomatoes, 160, *161*

Fennel

Braised Pork, and Lemon, Fusilli with, 174-75, *175*

Chickpeas, and Spinach, Fideos with, 184-85, *185*

and Saffron, Chicken and Potatoes with, 48, 49

Fideos with Chickpeas, Fennel, and Spinach, 184-85, *185*

Fish

Calamari, Chorizo, and Chickpea Stew, 102, *103*

Chowder, New England, 98-99, *99*

Haddock with Tomatoes, Escarole, and Crispy Garlic, 114-15, *115*

Halibut with Couscous and Ras el Hanout, 120-21, *121*

Halibut with Lentils, Kale, and Pancetta, 118-19, *119*

Swordfish Stew with Tomatoes, Capers, and Pine Nuts, *100*, 101

Swordfish with Braised Green Beans, Tomatoes, and Feta, 116-17, *117*

see also Salmon

G

Gai Lan, Soy Sauce Chicken with, 50-51, *51*

Garlic

Crispy, Tomatoes, and Escarole, Haddock with, 114-15, *115*

Everything Bagel Blend, 18

Harissa, 16

Ginger

Hawaiian Oxtail Soup, 66-67, *68-69*

-Miso Sauce, 15

-Orange Vinaigrette, 14

Ramen Noodles with Beef and Bok Choy, *190*, 191

Gochujang-Braised Tempeh Lettuce Wraps, 158, *159*

Grains

cooking instructions, 8

cook times, 9

see also specific grains

Green Bean(s)

Braised, Tomatoes, and Feta, Swordfish with, 116-17, *117*

and Chicken, Sweet and Savory Rice Noodles with, 188-89, *189*

Green Gumbo, 134, *135*

and Potato Salad, Warm, Steak Tips with, 72-73, *73*

Salmon Niçoise Salad, 104-5, *106-7*

Gumbo, Green, 134, *135*

H

Haddock with Tomatoes, Escarole, and Crispy Garlic, 114-15, *115*

Halibut

with Couscous and Ras el Hanout, 120-21, *121*

with Lentils, Kale, and Pancetta, 118-19, *119*

Harira, Chicken, 24, *25*

Harissa, 16

Hazelnut-Red Pepper Relish, Sherry-Braised Leeks on Toast with, 146-47, *147*

Herb(s)

-Yogurt Sauce, 17, *17*

see also specific herbs

Hominy

Pork Pozole Rojo, 82, *83*

I

Instant Pot

cooking beans and lentils in, 10

cooking foods in advance, 6

cooking proteins in, 12-13

cooking rice and grains in, 8-9

cooking vegetables, 11

helpful tips, 3

pressure release methods, 4

recipe instructions for, 4

troubleshooting, 5

useful tools, 3

J

Jambalaya, Shrimp, 126, *127*

Javaher Polo with Chicken, 40-41, *42-43*

Jicama Slaw, Shredded Beef Tacos with, 78-79, *79*

K

Kale

and Butternut Squash, Chicken and Barley Risotto with, 36-37, *37*

Lentils, and Pancetta, Halibut with, 118-19, *119*

and Manchego, Smoky Turkey Meatball Soup with, 28, *29*

Mushrooms, and Fontina, Spaghetti with, 176, *177*

L

Lamb

Abgoosht, 90-91, *92-93*

Meatballs with Creamy Lemon and Feta Orzo, 94-95, *95*

Leeks

Butternut Squash, and Burrata, Shells with, 182-83, *183*

and Mustard, Smothered Pork Chops with, 84-85, *85*

Sherry-Braised, on Toast with Red Pepper-Hazelnut Relish, 146-47, *147*

Lentils

Chicken Harira, 24, *25*

cooking instructions, 10

cook times, 10

Kale, and Pancetta, Halibut with, 118-19, *119*

and Tofu, Braised, with Thai Green Curry, *154*, 155

Lettuce Wraps, Gochujang-Braised Tempeh, 158, *159*

Lime-Sriracha Vinaigrette, 15, *15*

M

Mango Salsa, Shredded Chicken Tacos with, 56, 57

Meatball(s)

Lamb, with Creamy Lemon and Feta Orzo, 94-95, *95*

Smoky Turkey, Soup with Kale and Manchego, 28, *29*

Turkey, Spaghetti and, 168-69, *169*

Mint-Scallion Relish and Spiced Whole Parsnips, Chicken with, 46-47, *47*

Miso-Ginger Sauce, 15

Mushroom(s)

Braised Short Ribs with Daikon and Shiitakes, 74-75, *75*

Kale, and Fontina, Spaghetti with, 176, *177*

Ragù, Rigatoni with, 180-81, *181*

Sautéed Wild, Savory Oatmeal with, 164-65, *165*

Sweet Potato Glass Noodles with Portobellos and Spinach, 192-93, *193*

Mussels with Red Curry and Coconut Rice, 128-29, *129*

N

Noodle(s)

Chicken Soup with Shells, Tomatoes, and Zucchini, *22*, 23

Ginger Ramen, with Beef and Bok Choy, *190*, 191

Rice, Sweet and Savory, with Chicken and Green Beans, 188-89, *189*

Noodle(s) (*cont.*)

Sweet Potato Glass, with Portobellos and Spinach, 192-93, *193*

O

Oat Berry and Shrimp Bowl, Southwestern, 122-23, *123*

Oatmeal, Savory, with Sautéed Wild Mushrooms, 164-65, *165*

Okra

Green Gumbo, 134, *135*

Shrimp Jambalaya, 126, *127*

Olives

Boneless Short Ribs and Cauliflower Puttanesca, 76-77, *77*

and Prunes, Chicken and Couscous with, 52-53, *53*

Salmon Niçoise Salad, 104-5, *106-7*

Orange

-Ginger Vinaigrette, 14

and Wild Rice Salad, Salmon with, 110-11, *111*

P

Paprika

Harissa, 16

Rice, Smoky, with Crispy Artichokes and Peppers, 162-63, *163*

Parsley

-Pepita Sauce, Pork and Bulgur Bowls with, 86-87, *87*

Zhoug, 143, *145*

Parsnips, Spiced Whole, and
Scallion-Mint Relish, Chicken
with, 46-47, *47*
Pasta
Chicken Noodle Soup with
Shells, Tomatoes, and
Zucchini, *22, 23*
Creamy Spring Vegetable
Linguine, *178,* 179
Fideos with Chickpeas, Fennel,
and Spinach, 184-85, *185*
Fusilli with Braised Pork, Fennel,
and Lemon, 174-75, *175*
Lamb Meatballs with Creamy
Lemon and Feta Orzo, 94-95, *95*
Parmesan Penne with Chicken
and Asparagus, 170-71, *172-73*
Rigatoni with Mushroom Ragù,
180-81, *181*
Shells with Butternut Squash,
Leeks, and Burrata, 182-83, *183*
Sopa Seca with Chorizo and
Black Beans, 186-87, *187*
Spaghetti and Turkey Meatballs,
168-69, *169*
Spaghetti with Mushrooms,
Kale, and Fontina, 176, *177*
see also Couscous; Noodle(s)
Peanut-Sesame Sauce, 15
Peas
Green Gumbo, 134, *135*
Green Shakshuka, 140-41, *141*
Snap, Asparagus, and Tomatoes,
Farro Salad with, 160, *161*
Pepita(s)
or Sunflower Seeds, Spiced,
18, *18*
-Parsley Sauce, Pork and Bulgur
Bowls with, 86-87, *87*
Pepper(s)
and Artichokes, Crispy, Smoky
Paprika Rice with, 162-63, *163*

Pepper(s) (*cont.*)
Red, -Hazelnut Relish, Sherry-
Braised Leeks on Toast with,
146-47, *147*
see also Chiles
Pesto, Classic Basil, 16, *16*
Pickled Vegetables, Quick-, 19
Pine Nuts, Tomatoes, and Capers,
Swordfish Stew with, *100,* 101
Polenta, Creamy Parmesan, with
Eggplant, Sausage, and
Tomatoes, 88-89, *89*
Pomegranate
-Honey Vinaigrette, 14, *14*
Javaher Polo with Chicken,
40-41, *42-43*
Pork
Braised, Fennel, and Lemon,
Fusilli with, 174-75, *175*
and Bulgur Bowls with Parsley-
Pepita Sauce, 86-87, *87*
Chops, Smothered, with Leeks
and Mustard, 84-85, *85*
Pozole Rojo, 82, *83*
see also Sausage(s)
Potato(es)
Abgoosht, 90-91, *92-93*
Caldo Verde, *80,* 81
and Chicken with Fennel and
Saffron, 48, *49*
and Green Bean Salad, Warm,
Steak Tips with, 72-73, *73*
New England Fish Chowder,
98-99, *99*
Salmon Niçoise Salad, 104-5,
106-7
Sweet, and Bean Chili, 138, *139*
Swordfish with Braised Green
Beans, Tomatoes, and Feta,
116-17, *117*
Proteins
cooking tips, 12
cook times, 13

Prunes and Olives, Chicken and
Couscous with, 52-53, *53*
Pumpkin Mole and Apple-
Cabbage Slaw, Braised Tofu
with, 156-57, *157*

R

Radishes
Braised, and Chicken with
Dukkah, 34-35, *35*
Braised Short Ribs with Daikon
and Shiitakes, 74-75, *75*
Raisins
Braised Tofu with Pumpkin Mole
and Apple-Cabbage Slaw,
156-57, *157*
Javaher Polo with Chicken,
40-41, *42-43*
Swordfish Stew with Tomatoes,
Capers, and Pine Nuts, *100,* 101
Rice
Black, and Chicken Bowl with
Peanut-Sesame Dressing,
54, *55*
Brown, and Black Beans,
150, 151
Coconut, and Red Curry,
Mussels with, 128-29, *129*
cooking instructions, 8
cook times, 9
Javaher Polo with Chicken,
40-41, *42-43*
Shrimp Jambalaya, 126, *127*
Smoky Paprika, with Crispy
Artichokes and Peppers,
162-63, *163*
Wild, and Coconut Soup,
Spiced, *136,* 137
Wild, and Orange Salad, Salmon
with, 110-11, *111*

Risotto, Barley, and Chicken with Butternut Squash and Kale, 36–37, *37*

S

Sage
  -Apple Cider Vinaigrette, 14
  and Butternut Squash, Shrimp and White Beans with, *124*, 125
Salads
  Chickpea and Arugula, Baba Ghanoush with, 142–43, *144–45*
  Farro, with Asparagus, Snap Peas, and Tomatoes, 160, *161*
  Salmon Niçoise, 104–5, *106–7*
  Spiced Chickpea, Cucumber, and Tomato, Salmon with, 108, *109*
  Warm Bread and Arugula, Chicken with, 30–31, *32–33*
  Warm Potato and Green Bean, Steak Tips with, 72–73, *73*
  White Bean and Sun-Dried Tomato, Seared Flank Steak with, 70–71, *71*
  Wild Rice and Orange, Salmon with, 110–11, *111*
Salmon
  Niçoise Salad, 104–5, *106–7*
  with Ponzu-Braised Eggplant, *112*, 113
  with Spiced Chickpea, Cucumber, and Tomato Salad, 108, *109*
  with Wild Rice and Orange Salad, 110–11, *111*
Sauces
  Chipotle-Yogurt, 17
  Classic Basil Pesto, 16

Sauces (*cont.*)
  Harissa, 16
  Herb-Yogurt, 17, *17*
  Miso-Ginger, 15
  Peanut-Sesame Sauce, 15
  Tahini-Yogurt, 17
  Zhoug, 143, *145*
Sausages, Chicken, with White Beans and Spinach, 58, 59
Sausage(s)
  Calamari, Chorizo, and Chickpea Stew, 102, *103*
  Caldo Verde, *80*, 81
  Eggplant, and Tomatoes, Creamy Parmesan Polenta with, 88–89, *89*
  Shrimp Jambalaya, 126, *127*
  Sopa Seca with Chorizo and Black Beans, 186–87, *187*
Scallion-Mint Relish and Spiced Whole Parsnips, Chicken with, 46–47, 47
Seeds
  Everything Bagel Blend, 18
  Peanut-Sesame Sauce, 15
  Sunflower, or Pepitas, Spiced, 18, *18*
Shakshuka, Green, 140–41, 141
Shallots, Crispy, 18
Shellfish. *See* **Mussels; Shrimp**
Shrimp
  Jambalaya, 126, *127*
  and Oat Berry Bowl, Southwestern, 122–23, *123*
  and White Beans with Butternut Squash and Sage, *124*, 125
Sopa Seca with Chorizo and Black Beans, 186–87, 187
Soups
  Caldo Verde, *80*, 81
  Chicken Harira, 24, *25*
  Chicken Noodle, with Shells, Tomatoes, and Zucchini, *22*, 23

Soups (*cont.*)
  Hearty Minestrone, *132*, 133
  New England Fish Chowder, 98–99, *99*
  Oxtail, Hawaiian, 66–67, *68–69*
  Pork Pozole Rojo, 82, *83*
  Smoky Turkey Meatball, with Kale and Manchego, 28, *29*
  Spiced Wild Rice and Coconut, *136*, 137
Spinach
  Calamari, Chorizo, and Chickpea Stew, 102, *103*
  Chickpeas, and Fennel, Fideos with, 184–85, *185*
  Green Gumbo, 134, *135*
  Green Shakshuka, 140–41, *141*
  and Portobellos, Sweet Potato Glass Noodles with, 192–93, *193*
  and White Beans, Chicken Sausages with, *58*, 59
Squash
  Braised Tofu with Pumpkin Mole and Apple-Cabbage Slaw, 156–57, *157*
  Butternut, and Kale, Chicken and Barley Risotto with, 36–37, *37*
  Butternut, and Sage, Shrimp and White Beans with, *124*, 125
  Butternut, Leeks, and Burrata, Shells with, 182–83, *183*
  see also Zucchini
Sriracha-Lime Vinaigrette, 15, 15
Stews
  Abgoosht, 90–91, *92–93*
  Calamari, Chorizo, and Chickpea, 102, *103*
  Double Vegetable Beef, with Lemon Zest, 64–65, *65*
  Swordfish, with Tomatoes, Capers, and Pine Nuts, *100*, 101

Sunflower Seeds or Pepitas, Spiced, 18, *18*
Sweet Potato and Bean Chili, 138, *139*
Swiss chard
Green Shakshuka, 140-41, *141*
Lamb Meatballs with Creamy Lemon and Feta Orzo, 94-95, *95*
Spiced Wild Rice and Coconut Soup, *136*, 137
Swordfish
with Braised Green Beans, Tomatoes, and Feta, 116-17, *117*
Stew with Tomatoes, Capers, and Pine Nuts, *100*, 101

T

Tacos
Shredded Beef, with Jicama Slaw, 78-79, *79*
Shredded Chicken, with Mango Salsa, 56, *57*
Tahini-Yogurt Sauce, 17
Tempeh, Gochujang-Braised, Lettuce Wraps, 158, *159*
Tofu
Braised, with Pumpkin Mole and Apple-Cabbage Slaw, 156-57, *157*
and Lentils, Braised, with Thai Green Curry, 154, *155*
Tomato(es)
Asparagus, and Snap Peas, Farro Salad with, 160, *161*
Bean and Sweet Potato Chili, 138, *139*
Boneless Short Ribs and Cauliflower Puttanesca, 76-77, *77*

Tomato(es) *(cont.)*
Braised Green Beans, and Feta, Swordfish with, 116-17, *117*
Capers, and Pine Nuts, Swordfish Stew with, *100,* 101
Chana Masala, 152-53, *153*
Chicken Harira, 24, *25*
Chickpea, and Cucumber Salad, Spiced, Salmon with, 108, *109*
Eggplant, and Sausage, Creamy Parmesan Polenta with, 88-89, *89*
Escarole, and Crispy Garlic, Haddock with, 114-15, *115*
Rigatoni with Mushroom Ragù, 180-81, *181*
Shells, and Zucchini, Chicken Noodle Soup with, *22,* 23
Spaghetti and Turkey Meatballs, 168-69, *169*
Spaghetti with Mushrooms, Kale, and Fontina, 176, *177*
Sun-Dried, and White Bean Salad, Seared Flank Steak with, 70-71, *71*
Turkey
Meatballs, Spaghetti and, 168-69, *169*
Meatball Soup, Smoky, with Kale and Manchego, 28, *29*

V

Vegetable(s)
cook times, 11
Double, Beef Stew with Lemon Zest, 64-65, *65*
Hearty Minestrone, *132*, 133
Mashed Root, Chicken in a Pot with, 60-61, *61*
Quick-Pickled, 19

Vegetable(s) *(cont.)*
Spring, Chicken with, 44-45, *45*
Spring, Linguine, Creamy, *178*, 179
see also specific vegetables
Vinaigrette. *See under* **Dressings**

W

Wild Rice
and Coconut Soup, Spiced, *136*, 137
and Orange Salad, Salmon with, 110-11, *111*

Y

Yogurt
-Chipotle Sauce, 17
-Herb Sauce, 17, *17*
Homemade, 19
-Tahini Sauce, 17

Z

Zhoug, 143, *145*
Zucchini
Hearty Minestrone, *132*, 133
Shells, and Tomatoes, Chicken Noodle Soup with, *22,* 23
White Chicken Chili with, 26-27, *27*